AMERICAN QUILTER'S SOCIETY

2010

Catalogue
of
SHOW QUILTS

Semi-finalists in the

26th Annual
AQS QUILT SHOW & CONTEST

PADUCAH KENTUCKY

Located in Paducah, Kentucky, the American Quilter's Society (AQS) is dedicated to promoting the accomplishments of today's quilters. Through its publications and events, AQS strives to honor today's quiltmakers and their work and to inspire future creativity and innovation in quiltmaking.

Artwork © 2010, American Quilter's Society

EXECUTIVE EDITOR: ANDI MILAM REYNOLDS
EDITOR: BONNIE K. BROWNING
GRAPHIC DESIGN: ELAINE WILSON
COVER DESIGN: MICHAEL BUCKINGHAM
PHOTOGRAPHY: SUPPLIED BY THE INDIVIDUAL QUILTMAKERS

American Quilter's Society
P. O. Box 3290 • Paducah, KY 42002-3290
www.AmericanQuilter.com

Additional copies of this book may be ordered from the American Quilter's Society, PO Box 3290, Paducah, KY 42002-3290, or online at www.AmericanQuilter.com.

Proudly printed and bound in the United States of America

April 21–24, 2010 is the 26th Annual AQS Quilt Show & Contest in Paducah, Kentucky. More than $120,000 will be awarded to the winners of this year's contest, with the Janome Best of Show winner receiving $20,000. More than 500 quilts will on display at the show.

Quilters from 47 U.S. states and 10 countries entered quilts this year. The 387 quilts in the quilt contest represent a variety of techniques, from traditional piecing and appliqué to innovative use of threads, paint, embroidery, and other embellishments.

Make your plans now to enter the 27th Annual AQS Quilt Show & Contest in 2011.

Meredith Schroeder

Meredith Schroeder
AQS President and Founder

CATEGORY NUMBERS — CATEGORY

BED QUILTS

100s	Hand Quilted	4
200s	Home Sewing Machine	11
300s	Longarm/Midarm Machine	13
400s	1st Entry in an AQS Quilt Contest	17
500s	Group	23

LARGE WALL QUILTS

600s	Hand Quilted	26
700s	Home Sewing Machine	34
800s	Longarm/Midarm Machine	42
900s	Pictorial Quilts	49

SMALL WALL QUILTS

1000s	Hand Quilted	54
1100s	Home Sewing Machine	59
1200s	Longarm/Midarm Machine	71
1300s	Pictorial Quilts	76
1400s	1st Entry in an AQS Quilt Contest	87

| 1500s | **MINIATURE QUILTS** | 94 |

	INDEX OF QUILTMAKERS	101
	INDEX OF QUILTS	104
	CONTEST RULES	108
	2010 QUILT SHOW SPONSORS	110

101. FOREVER SPRING, 109" x 119"
Annabel Baugher, Trenton, MO

102. MURPHY'S STAR, 84" x 85"
Linda Dyken, Mobile, AL

103. A WELCOME PRESENT, 80" x 87"
Junko Fujiwara, Narashino City, Chiba, Japan

104. FLOWERS IN AQUA, 85" x 85"
Kumiko Funaki, Saitama City, Saitama, Japan

Cottage Charm pattern from *American Patchwork & Quilting® Magazine*; BHG, August 2007; Becky Hanks workshop

Keiko Miyauchi workshop

Arab Tent pattern from *1001 Patchwork Designs*© 1982 by Maggie Malone. Used with permission from Sterling Publishing, Co., Inc.

Block patterns from *Butterflies in the Garden* by Pat Andreatta, Heirloom Stitches, 1992

Tropical Birds Coloring Book by Lucia deLeiris, Dover Publications, Inc., 1984

105. Butterflies in the Garden, 95" x 95"
Peggy Garwood, Fairfield Glade, TN

106. Tropical Beauty, 85" x 85"
Donna Gilbert, Fayetteville, PA

107. Harmony, 76" x 80" Hatsune Hirano
Honjo, Saitama, Japan

108. Honey, I'm Home, 101" x 110"
Hope Johnson, Shelburne, VT

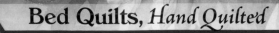

Kathy Nakajima workshop

109. My Favorite Monstera, 94" x 94"
Yachiyo Katsuno, Setagaya, Tokyo, Japan

110. Stars Over Agrabah, 76" x 83"
Kathy Kelley, Waco, TX

111. The Endless World II, 73" x 91"
Noriko Kido, Nagoya, Aichi, Japan

112. Sew is Life, 102" x 102"
Barbara Korengold, Chevy Chase, MD

Baltimore Appliqué Society patterns from *The DAR Museum Introduces the Mary Simon Quilt Top*© BALTIMORE ALBUM QUILT, 2002-2003, based on c. 1846 original cotton, polyester 110 x 125 x 5 in. Reproduction of the Samuel Williams Album Quilt (BMA 1988.206) by the Baltimore Appliqué Society; Lovely Lane Museum 150th/50th Anniversary Quilt Patterns, Lovely Lane Museum and Archives, Baltimore, MD

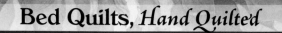

Keiko Miyauchi workshop

Kathy Nakajima design

113. Chorus of Angels, 86" x 86"
Masako Kumagawa, Agatsuma, Gunma, Japan

114. Laced Lokelani, 82" x 82"
Yoshiko Maezawa, Miura, Kanagawa, Japan

115. I Love Waikiki, 82" x 82"
Takako Miyake, Ibaraki, Osaka, Japan

116. Animal Book, 70" x 85"
Megumi Mizuno, Shiki, Saitama, Japan

Kathy Nakajima design

Whimsical Animals Illustrations CD-ROM and Book, Dover Publications, Inc., 2000

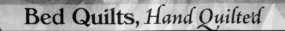

117. KOMOREBI, 82" x 82"
Shizuyo Morishita, Ota, Tokyo, Japan

118. GRADATION LOG CABIN #7, 89" x 89"
Fumiko Ohkawa, Kobe, Hyogo, Japan

119. PRECIOUS HOPES, 80" x 80"
Miki Ozaki, Tatsuno, Hyogo, Japan

120. RETURN TO THE ATTIC, 100" x 100"
Marsha D. Radtke, Crossville, TN

Kathy Nakajima design

A 'Baltimore' Album: 25 Appliqué Patterns by Marsha D. Radtke, American Quilter's Society, 2009

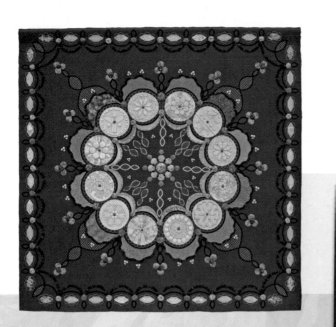

121. VINTAGE BUTTON BOUQUET, 83" x 83"
Linda Roy, Knoxville, TN

122. FLOATING LILIES ALONG THE WATER
86" x 86" Akemi Sugyama, Hamura, Tokyo, Japan

123. SPECIAL ROSE, 80" x 80"
Fusako Takido, Shizuoka City, Shizuoka, Japan

124. IN MY GARDEN, 88" x 88"
Nadine Thompson, Springfield, MO

Thru Grandmother's Window Block-of-the-Month ePatterns by Becky Goldsmith
and Linda Jenkins, ©Piece O'Cake Designs

Keiko Miyauchi workshop

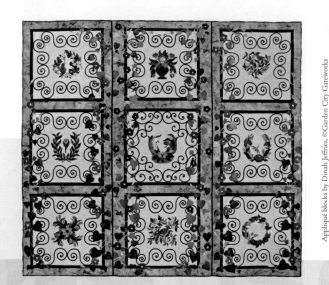

Appliqué blocks by Dinah Jeffries, ©Garden City Gateworks

125. Roses of Shenandoah, 89" x 89"
Rita Verroca, Westlake Village, CA

126. Morning Glory Madness, 99" x 89",
Joann Webb, Grain Valley, MO

127. Radiant Flowers, 86" x 86"
Naoko Yamada, Tajimi, Gifu, Japan

128. Hibiscus in Hawaiian Breeze, 84" x 89"
Yoko Yamamoto, Takarazuka, Hyogo, Japan

Kathy Nakajima design

Square-in-a-Square design from *Quilt* magazine, Summer 1988

Friendship's Garden pattern from *Friendship's Garden: Quilts and Projects* by Blackbird Designs, by Alma Allen and Cheri Ralston, Blackbird Designs, LLC, 2003

201. IN PRAISE OF WOOL, 76" x 86"
Mary Chalmers, Willmar, MN

202. SEVEN BLACK BIRDS, 84" x 84"
Sandra H. Gilreath, Bonaire, GA

203. RED AND GREEN REDUX, 82" x 102"
Lynn Isenberg, Saint Louis, MO

204. WEDDING RINGS FOR MAVIS AND CJ
96" x 108", Fran Kordek, Elkins, WV

205. CROWNING GLORY, 76" x 95"
Julie Yaeger Lambert, Erlanger, KY

206. HIBISCUS, 86" x 86"
Jean Lohmar, Galesburg, IL

207. THE FESTIVAL OF THE NIGHT SKY
82" x 93" Kazuko Noto, Akita City, Akita, Japan

208. CUTWORK APPLIQUÉ, 104" x 104"
Jerre Reese, Murrells Inlet, SC

Dear Jane: The Two Hundred Twenty-five Patterns from the 1863 Jane A. Stickle Quilt by Brenda Manges Papadakis, www.dearjane.com. EZ Quilting by Wrights, 1996

209. Jeepers...It's Jane!, 80" x 86"
Beth Schillig, Columbus, OH

210. Charisma, 84" x 84"
Mildred Sorrells, Macomb, IL

211. My Kind of Fun, 69" x 86"
Vicki Spiering, Wauwatosa, WI

301. Joyful Journey, 82" x 82"
Barbara Black, Huntsville, AL

Inspired by a Ruth B. Smalley quilt

Washington Medallion ©Susan H. Garman

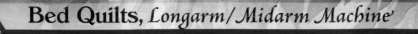

Reproduction of an 1848 quilt found in Virginia

302. SYNCHRONIZED DANCE, 84" x 83"
Irena Bluhm, Antlers, OK

303. M.E.C. REMEMBERED, 91" x 91"
Barbara M. Burnham, Ellicott City, MD

304. MOUNTAIN HOLLY AND THE RARE RED-BERRIED MISTLETOE, 84" x 84",
Jan Cunningham, Acworth, GA

305. BIRDS 'N URNS, 95" x 95"
Kathy Delaney, Overland Park, KS

Holly & Mistletoe pattern from *When the Cold Wind Blows: Quilts and Projects to Keep You Warm* by Barb Adams and Alma Allen, Kansas City Star Books, 2008; Sharon Schamber's machine-appliqué method

Inspired by a Nancy Page Quilt Club series quilt from the 1930s

Blocks from *Birds of a Feather* by Barb Adams and Alma Allen of Blackbird Designs, Kansas City Star Books, 2006

306. BIRDS OF A FEATHER, 69" x 82"
Darlene Donohue, Hilton Head Island, SC

307. JESUS, THE TRUE VINE
88" x 88", Cindy Garcia, Racine, WI

308. GALAXY OF NOSTALGIC SNAILS
94" x 94", Elisabeth Polenz Haase, Weston, WI

309. LATTE OBSESSION, 96" x 96"
Janet Knapp, Fergus Falls, MN

Inspired by Shakespeare in the Park from *The Creative Pattern Book* © 2000 Judy Martin, Crosley-Griffith Publishing Company, Inc.

Latte Quilt by Kerrie Hay, Quilters' Resource Publications, 2002

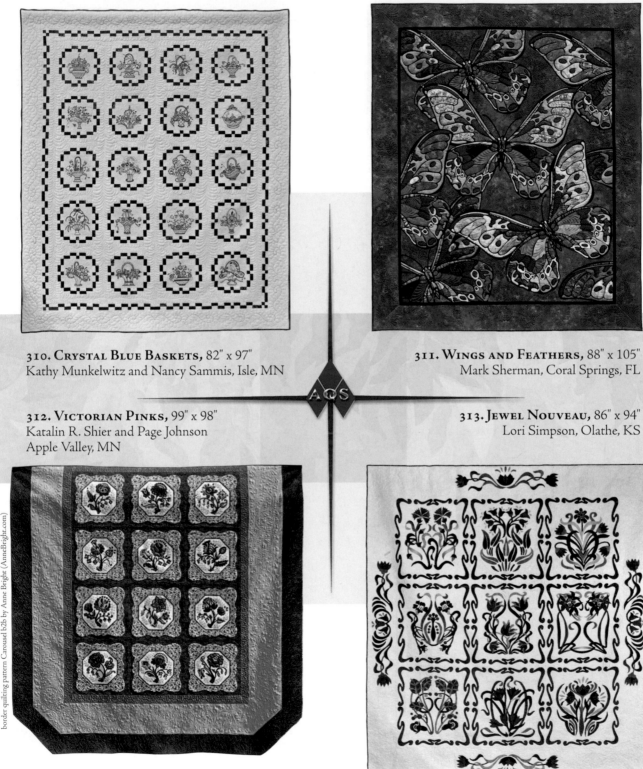

Vintage Kansas City Star and Aunt Martha's patterns

Designs for Coloring: *Butterflies*, written and illustrated by Ruth Heller, ©Penguin Young Readers Group, Penguin Group (USA) Inc.

By G~: It's Blue collection by Jeni Buechel ©2001, ornamentalAppliqué; border quilting pattern Carousel b2b by Anne Bright (AnneBright.com)

Rhapsody in Bloom pattern by Suzanne Marshall

310. Crystal Blue Baskets, 82" x 97"
Kathy Munkelwitz and Nancy Sammis, Isle, MN

311. Wings and Feathers, 88" x 105"
Mark Sherman, Coral Springs, FL

312. Victorian Pinks, 99" x 98"
Katalin R. Shier and Page Johnson
Apple Valley, MN

313. Jewel Nouveau, 86" x 94"
Lori Simpson, Olathe, KS

Pattern from *Creative Expressions with Jenny Haskins Special Edition: Moulin Rouge.* Nov. 2004

314. JUST BECAUSE REVISITED, 66" x 82"
Kristin Vierra, Lincoln, NE

315. MOULIN ROUGE, 73" x 100"
Charlotte Wright, Stillwater, OK

401. ISTANBUL'S FLOWER, 80" x 80"
Hisae Abe, Katsushika, Tokyo, Japan

402. BELLA ROSE, 84" x 84"
Bobbie Ashley, Schertz, TX

Keiko Miyauchi workshop

Tree of Paradise block from *More Quilts from The Quiltmaker's Gift* by Joanne Larsen Line, Scholastic/Orchard Books, copyright© 2003

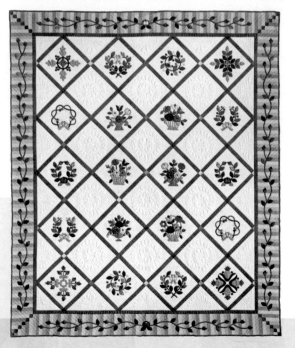

Mimi Dietrich's *Baltimore Basics: Album Quilts from Start to Finish*, That Patchwork Place®, 2006

403. 322 Treehouse Lane, 87" x 87"
Cindy Behrens, Waukesha, WI

404. Challenge I, 74" x 90"
Georgina Buschauer, Houston, TX

405. Colorwash Garden, 90" x 90"
Clara Cartwright, Shell Knob, MO

406. Bloomin Beauty, 102" x 82"
Gail Eberle and Kristi Hawkins, Oakley, KS

Colorwash Garden Series by Rose M. Hahn, Hahn Enterprises

Double Stars pattern from *Favorites!* by Jackie Robinson, Animas Quilts Publishing, 2000; www.animasquilts.com; Irena Bluhm workshop

Feathered Fantasy pattern by Shirley Sturz, Quilt Collector Series

Flowers for Mackenzie pattern, ©From my heart to your hands: Quilt Designs by Lori Smith; *Think Small: Over 300 Miniature Quilting Designs* by Shirley Thompson, Golden Threads, 1990; *Fine Feathers: A Quilter's Guide* to (customizing Traditional Feather Quilting Designs by Marianne Fons, C&T Publishing, Inc., 1988; folded-rose technique from '*Baltimore Beauties and Beyond: Studies in Classic Album Quilt Appliqué* by Elly Sienkiewicz, C&T Publishing, Inc., 1989; piped-binding techniques by Susan K. Cleveland as published in *American Quilter*, 2005; Susan Bryan workshop

407. PAISLEYS AND PEACOCKS, INDIA REMEMBERED, 82" x 82" Sharon Hansen, McKeesport, PA

408. FLORAL BEAUTY, 91" x 91"
Mary M. Haukom, Colorado Springs, CO

409. FOUR SEASONS OF WONDERMENT
88" x 88", Gay Joyner, Big Bear Lake, CA

410. WOVEN-WIND FLOWERS, 92" x 99"
Dolores Keaton, Pacific, MO

Baskets, Baskets, Fruit & Flowers by Toni Phillips and Juanita Simonich, Fabric Expressions

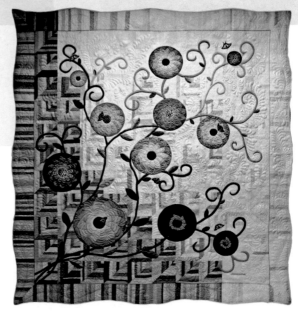

Tranquil Treasures pattern variation from *Strips and Strings: 16 Sparkling Quilts* by Evelyn Sloppy, That Patchwork Place®, 2003

Appliqué Masterpiece Little 'Brown Bird' Patterns by Margaret Docherty; American Quilter's Society, 2000; Appliqué Takes Wing; Exquisite 'Designs for 'Birds, Butterflies, and More' by Jane Townswick, That Patchwork Place®, 2005

Storybook Snugglers: Once 'Upon a 'Time' by Cheryl Almgren Taylor, The Patchwork Place®, 2007; Sew Easy Celtic: Designing Simplified, Appliqué 'Perfected' by Angela Madden, MCQ Pub., 1993; Celtic Quilts: A 'New Look' for Ancient 'Designs' by Beth Ann Williams, That Patchwork Place®, 2000; English Cottage pattern by Joan Statz, ©Joan's Own Creations

411. Brown Bird's Lullaby, 84" x 84"
Sally Magee, Heath, TX

412. Ye Ole Celtic Cottages, 87" x 92"
Karen S. Measels, Huntsville, AL

413. Sweet Candy Dots, 81" x 81"
Diana Napier, Mountain, WI

414. Blue Merle (Circle Log Cabin)
87" x 87" Keith A. Nuehring, Independence, IA

Armenian Tiles pattern by Liz Schwartz and Stephen Seifert from "Quilts with Style", Sept./Oct. 2007, www.eequiltpatterns.com

415. RAINBOW PYRAMID, 82" x 94"
Katheryn Peck, Fairfield, IA

416. REYNOLDS CROSSING, 108" x 108"
Sherry Reynolds, Laramie, WY

417. BLOSSOM OF MY LIFE, 84" x 83"
Taeko Shinozaki, Shibuya, Tokyo, Japan

418. FIRST WE TAKE MANHATTAN
80" x 80", Carole Sorrell, Auckland,
New Zealand

Lady Liberty Goes to Hawaii pattern from *Karen K. Stone Quilts*, The Electric Quilt ® Company, 2004

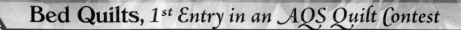

419. THE COLOR OF MATSURI (JAPANESE FESTIVAL), 95" x 95", Mitsuyo Takasaki, Utsunomiya, Tochigi, Japan

420. MORNING SUNSHINE, 69" x 86"
Natsuko Tsukatani, Kobe, Hyogo, Japan

421. SIMPLY MANDALAS, 90" x 90"
Pierra Vernex, Saint-Jerome, Quebec, Canada

422. CIRCLE PARADE, 81" x 81"
Akiko Watanabe, Nagano, Nagano, Japan

300 Patchwork Patterns by Chuck Nohara, Japan Vogue, 2001

Star Sapphire block from "Patchwork Portfolio: A Presentation of 165 Original Quilt Designs by Jinny Beyer, Howell Press, Inc., 1990

Quilting the Garden by Barb Adams, Alma Allen and Ricki Creamer, Kansas City Star Books

Floral Bouquet designed by Shirley and Shirlene Wedd, Sunflower Pattern Cooperative. Barbara Brackman

423. FLOWER SEEDS OF HAPPINESS
83" x 83", Yasue Watanabe, Yokohama, Kanagawa, Japan

424. FLORENTINE WINDOW, 93" x 93"
Debi Webb, Hedgesville, WV

501. ALWAYS A BLOOM IN MY GARDEN
84" x 84", Hazel Ashworth, Fargo, ND

502. MARYLAND BEAUTY, 106" x 109"
Bethesda Quilters, Glen Echo, MD

503. FISH OF RAINBOW COLORS, 98" x 98"
Cherry Basket, Maebashi, Gunma, Japan

505. CAMELLIA OF ART DECO, 80" x 80"
Junko Sawada Group, Yokohama, Kanagawa,
Japan

504. VARSITY MEDLEY, 101" x 101"
Joanne Coughlin, Helen Fisher, and the
Second Friday Quilters, Ann Arbor, MI

506. AUTUMN SPLENDOUR, 90" x 111"
Kingston Heirloom Quilters, Kingston,
Ontario, Canada

Varsity Medley pattern from Knockout Blocks and Sampler Quilts, ©2004 Judy
Martin, Crosley-Griffith Publishing Company, Inc.

New Beginnings/Expanding Friendships by Carolyn Abbott from *American Quilter Ultimate Projects,*
2004

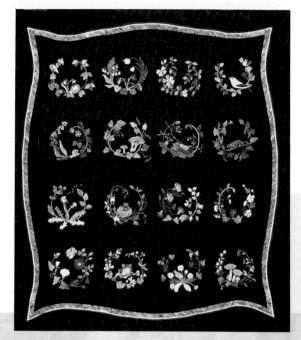

A Walk in the Meadow pattern by Ellen Heck

Based on the *Rising Sun* quilt by Mary Betsy Totten, ca. 1830, the Smithsonian collection

507. A Walk in the Meadow, 70" x 80"
Lou Ann McVay & Meri Pinner, Stigler, OK

508. Indiana Starburst, 80" x 80"
Judy Laval Morton, Lydia Stoll and
Miriam Graber, Newburgh, IN

509. Mother-Daughter Redwork
71" x 88", Barbara Polston, Phoenix, AZ

510. Hawaiian Cross, 77" x 96"
Yukiko Tareishi and Friends
Yamagata City, Yamagata, Japan

Starring Red & White pattern from Lace Tales Embroidery

Kathy Nakajima design

601. FOREST WALKS, 78" x 78"
Tomoko Arai, Tsuruoka, Yamagata, Japan

602. FLYING, 63" x 74" , Yeung Ran Choung
Busan, South Korea

603. MEMORIES, 76" x 56"
Karen Fitch, Union City, PA

604. GLORY OF ANCIENT REMAINS, 70" x 62
Hiroko Goda, Niihama, Ehime, Japan

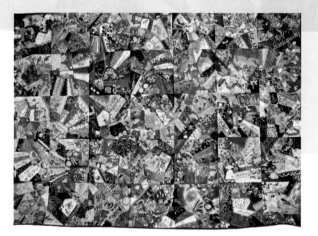

Ricky Tims Rhapsody workshop

Designs from *Take Away Appliqué* by Suzanne Marshall, American Quilter's Society, 1998

Keiko Miyauchi workshop

Eyelet Edging border pattern from *Appliqué Lace Patterns* by Linda Pool, American Quilter's Society, 2006; Noriko Masui workshop

605. Cwlwm Lafant, 82" x 82"
Gwenfai Rees Griffiths, Abergele,
North Wales, United Kingdom

607. Rondo of Roses, 61" x 68"
Mieko Hara, Fukui City, Fukui, Japan

606. All Creatures Great & Small
82" x 64", Karen L. Guthrie, Marshall, MO

608. Galaxy, 69" x 69", Kayoko Hata
Yokohama, Kanagawa, Japan

Noriko Masui workshop

609. A Breath of Spring, 77" x 77"
Akemi Hirasawa, Setagaya, Tokyo, Japan

610. Development, 80" x 80"
Yuriko Ikuma, Hamamatsu, Shizuoka, Japan

611. Anniversary, 80" x 80"
Kyoko Inagaki, Osaka City, Osaka, Japan

612. Blue Land, 66" x 66", Ikuyo Kitada
Yokohama, Kanagawa, Japan

Noriko Masui workshop

613. Tamoto huri huri, 63" x 78"
Yoshiko Kitami, Inabe, Mie, Japan

614. Tale of a Korean Thimble Golmu
65" x 78" Chungsu Lee, Seongnam,
Gyeonggi, South Korea

615. Dream Land, 71" x 71"
Shizuyo Morishita, Ota, Tokyo, Japan

616. Whimsey, 80" x 80"
Kathy Munkelwitz, Isle, MN

Noriko Masui workshop

617. The Coming of Spring, 89" x 89"
Mariko Nakano, Yotsukaido, Chiba, Japan

618. Flower Carnival, 76" x 76"
Yukiko Nakao, Ryugasaki, Ibaraki, Japan

619. My Lovely Susie, 83" x 83"
Hitomi Oiwa, Ashikaga, Tochigi, Japan

620. Beyond Sky, 82" x 81"
Chizuko Okamoto, Nagoya, Aichi, Japan

Inspiration from Susie Cooper® teacup designs

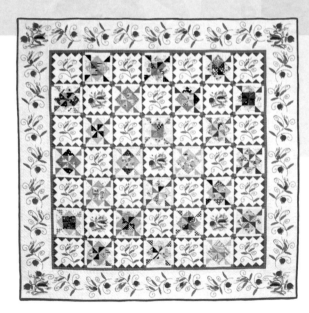

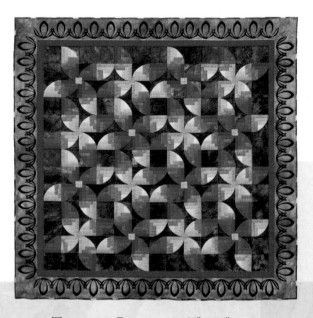

621. Tropical Beauties, 65" x 65"
Hallie H. O'Kelley, Tuscaloosa, AL

622. The Concerto in the Night Sky
78" x 78", Uiko Onuma, Kodaira, Tokyo, Japan

623. For All My Companions
68" x 68", Mariko Oosawa, Miyagigun,
Miyagi, Japan

624. Walk in the Forest, 69" x 69"
Norde Sebens, Sierra Vista, AZ

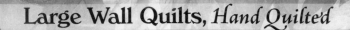

Noriko Masui workshop

625. 25TH WEDDING ANNIVERSARY
71" x 71", Mitsuko Sutoh, Sendai
Miyagi, Japan

626. BRIGHT FUTURE OF DAUGHTERS
69" x 69" Yuko Takahashi, Shimotsuga,
Tochigi, Japan

627. SWEET BOUQUET, 79" x 86",
Kyoko Takemoto, Naganoshi City,
Nagano, Japan

**628. THE SWEET MEMORIES ARE FOREVER
IN MY HEART,** 78" x 79", Yasuko Takeyama
Higashihiroshima, Hiroshima, Japan

Phoenix pattern by Takemoto Youhei; quilt design by Felisa Nakazawa

Noriko Masu workshop

629. Passion, 70" x 70"
Junko Tanaka, Hiratsuka, Kanagawa, Japan

630. Fruit of the Loom, 70" x 70"
Teri Henderson Tope, Worthington, OH

631. Healing Rose Hip, 78" x 78"
Kinuko Tsuchiya, Kitakatsushika
Saitama, Japan

632. Dream Story, 78" x 78"
Yoshimi Umemoto, Funabashi, Chiba, Japan

Keiko Miyauchi workshop

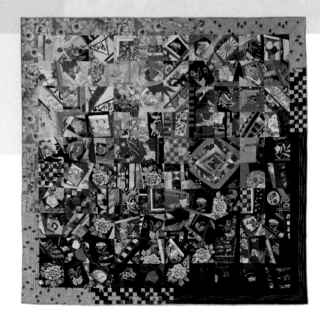

633. ROSE AND STAR WALTZ, 72" x 72"
Kayoko Yamamoto, Chiba City, Chiba, Japan

701. ORIENTAL DAHLIA, 78" x 78"
Tajima Akemi, Hiki, Saitana, Japan

702. SUNSHINE & SHADOW, 76" x 75"
Esther Aliu, Donvale, Victoria, Australia

703. FLOWER & BIRDS I, 61" x 61",
Eun Young Choi, Seongnam,
Gyeonggi, South Korea

The Design Book by Japan Vogue

Based on designs from 3rd Exhibition of Kim Hyun Hee Embroidery & Pojagi Institute; Kim Hyun Hee, Seoul, 2006

704. Monsteriosity, 64" x 48"
Jan Frazer, Elwood, Victoria, Australia

705. Fractal Blue Rose, 78" x 78"
Kumiko Funaki, Saitama City, Saitama, Japan

706. Multiple Personalities
67" x 78", Cindi Goodwin, Naples, FL

707. Bouquet for Mr. Tims, 77" x 42"
Patti Hempen, Canyon Lake, TX

Bird pattern from Made in Mexico Block-of-the-Month collection, ©J. Michelle Watts

708. Ballet, 64" x 84"
Dianne S. Hire, Northport, ME

709. Glittering Summer Garden, 76" x 73"
Noriko Hosoo, Yokohama, Kanagawa, Japan

710. Precious Moments, 71" x 76"
Katsumi Ishinami, Iwakuni, Yamaguchi, Japan

711. Playing Rats, 65" x 73"
Kumiko Itoyama, Sendai, Miyagi, Japan

New York Beauty by Karen K. Stone. K. K. Stone, 1995

Inspired by Bethany Reynolds' Stack-n-Whack® technique

712. Black Lace, 79" x 79"
Jolana A. Jordan, Great Falls, VA

713. Snowball's Chance, 66" x 66"
Georgianne Kandler and Sharon Murphy
Arroyo Grande, CA

714. Aquatic Circles, 68" x 68"
Masae Kashizaki, Yokohama, Kanagawa, Japan

715. Pueblo Rain, 81" x 59"
Shirley P. Kelly, Colden, NY

Keep on Quilting Pattern Pack #1 by Keryn Emmerson, Golden Threads;
Yoko Ueda workshop

Inspired by Hopi, Zuni and Navajo motifs

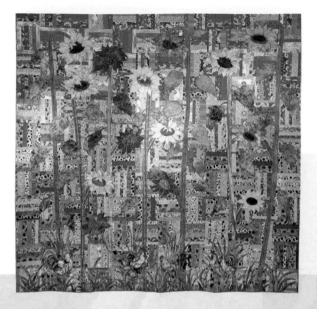

716. Sunflowers, 98" x 98"
LuAnn Kessi, Eddyville, OR

717. Pink Petal Party, 73" x 73"
Susan Brubaker Knapp, Mooresville, NC

718. Tea with Miss D, 71" x 71"
Sandra Leichner, Albany, OR

719. New York, New York, 70" x 80"
Jan Lewis, Grand Rapids, MI

New York Beauty by Karen K. Stone, 1995

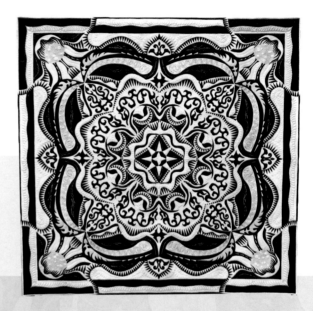

720. TREASURES IN THE SEA, 82" x 53"
Nancy Sterett Martin, Owensboro, KY

721. SOLEIL, 77" x 77", Felisa Nakazawa
Ueda, Nagano, Japan

722. WHITE GOLD, 84" x 83" Philippa Naylor
Beverley, East Yorkshire, United Kingdom

723. ON SPACESHIP, 72" x 67"
Taeko Okamatsu, Hino, Tokyo, Japan

Inspired by *The Little Prince* by Antoine de Saint-Exupéry, Mariner Books, 2000

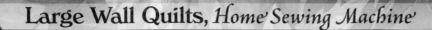
Based on a tissue artwork Easter mural by Harold R. Muller

724. Morning Has Broken, 75" x 76"
Peggy Parrott, Lakewood, CO

Cinco de Mayo pattern from *Karen K. Stone Quilts* by Karen K. Stone,
The Electric Quilt® Company, 2004

725. This Old Thing, 72" x 72"
Elaine Wick Poplin, Huntsville, AL

The "Bucking Horse and Rider" logo is a registered trademark of the State of Wyoming, used with permission

726. My Wyoming Valley, 67" x 67"
Sherry Reynolds, Laramie, WY

727. Calendula, 66" x 66"
Mary C. Schroeder, North Bend, OR

728. Clam Session, 61" x 61"
Karen K. Stone, Beaumont, TX

729. Between the Lines, 74" x 91"
Carol Taylor, Pittsford, NY

730. Colorado Sunrise Sunset
80" x 80", Katie Wells, Denver, CO

731. Miraflores, 68" x 45"
Sandra C. Werlich, Carbondale, IL

Hawaiian Star pattern, ©Judy Niemeyer, Quiltworx.com

732. MOONDANCE, 66" x 86"
Melanie West, Baton Rouge, LA

733. TROPICAL RADIANCE, 64" x 64"
Rachel Wetzler, St. Charles, IL

734. CAMP FIRE, 61" x 59"
Eunhee Woo, Busan, South Korea

801. WHAT WILL BE, WILL BE!
68" x 57", Sheila D. Blair, Atlanta, GA

Judy B. Dales design; Jean Richardson workshops

BQ pattern by Debbie Bowles, Maple Island Quilts

Reynola Pakusich workshop

802. SEASONS, 61" x 79"
Michele Byrum and Laurel Keith, Salem, OR

803. ORIENTAL FANTASY, 62" x 62"
Dot Collins, Port Neches, TX

804. REMEMBERING ROSE, 80" x 80"
Peg Collins, Alamosa, CO

805. SUNDANCE, 70" x 72"
Debra Crine, Marco Island, FL

Inspired by the ORCHID WREATH quilt by Rose Frances Good Kretsinger, 1928, 1971.0094, from the collection of the Spencer Museum of Art, The University of Kansas, Lawrence.

Phat Tuesday pattern, ©Deb Karasik, www.Quiltmavens.com

Amelia's Rose Garden Block-of-the-Month collection, ©Verna Mosquera,
The Vintage Spool

806. My Rose Garden, 66" x 66"
Rosemary Cushman, Sanford, NC

807. Listen with Your Eyes, 78" x 78"
Jacqueline de Jonge, Delft, ZH, The Netherlands

808. Doormats #1, 67" x 49"
Marcia DeCamp, Palmyra, NY

809. Papercuts and Toile, 68" x 68"
Kathy Delaney, Overland Park, KS

Inspired by patterns from *Winning Stitches: Hand Quilting Secrets, 50 Fabulous Designs, Quilts to Make by* Elsie M. Campbell, C&T Publishing, Inc., 2004

810. Hearts & Flowers, 78" x 78"
Terri Doyle, Gilbert, AZ

811. iCandy 3.0, 67" x 67"
Robbi Joy Eklow, Third Lake, IL

812. Autumn Joy, 67" x 78"
Gina Elias, Spring Valley, IL

813. Garden Frost, 79" x 97"
Patricia Johnson and Dawn Cavanaugh
West Des Moines, IA

Appliqué with Folded Cutwork by Anita Shackelford, American Quilter's Society, 1999

Aunt Millie's Garden: 12 Flowering Blocks from Piece O' Cake Designs by Becky Goldsmith and Linda Jenkins, C&T Publishing, Inc., 2008; Angela Lawrence workshop

Inspired by J. R. R. Tolkien's *The Lord of the Rings* and the film adaptation by Peter Jackson

Hawaiian Quilting: Instructions and Full-Size Patterns for 20 Blocks by Elizabeth Root, Dover Publications, Inc., 1989

814. TRIBUTE TO TOLKIEN, 85" x 90"
Sue McCarty, Roy, UT

815. JOURNEYS, 82" x 82"
Margaret McDonald and Susan Campbell
Lockwood South, Victoria, Australia

816. THE BIG BANG, 76" x 76"
Linda McGibbon, Beaverton, MI

817. HELL FREEZES OVER, 73" x 86"
Claudia Clark Myers and Marilyn Badger
Duluth, MN

818. Tuscan Sun, 86" x 64"
Gina Perkes, Payson, AZ

819. The Sampler, 67" x 81"
Barbara Persing, Frederick, PA

820. Flowing Counterpoint
61" x 62", Leslie Rego, Sun Valley, ID

821. Resurrection of Spring
78" x 78", Sharyl Schlieckau
Loganville, WI

Variation of Blooming Nine-Patch pattern from *Tradition with a Twist: Variations on Your Favorite Quilts* by Blanche Young and Dalene Young Stone, C&T Publishing, Inc., 1996; digitized embroidery patterns by Zundt Design, zundtdesign.com

822. GLORIA'S GARDEN, 73" x 73"
Susan Stewart and Gloria Meyer
Pittsburg, KS

823. THE FRAGILE WORLD, 89" x 89"
Judy Woodworth, Gering, NE

824. DRAGON STAR, 62" x 62"
Sally Zimmer, Bark River, MI

825. FOREVER YOURS, 73" x 73"
Kathryn Zimmerman and Brian Fackler
Mars Hill, NC

Dragon Star pattern, ©Judy Niemeyer, Quiltworx.com

Embroidery designs from Jenny Haskins, Sue Box, and KennyKreations; Vintage Valentine pattern, © Verna Mosquera, The Vintage Spool

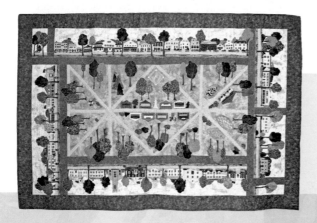

901. GUILFORD, CT, CA 1950, 95" x 65"
Brenda Archambault, Sun City West, AZ

902. MEDEA ESCAPING, 102" x 81"
Marilyn Belford, Chenango Forks, NY

903. FANTASY IN LACE, 82" x 88"
Mary S. Buvia, Greenwood, IN

904. THE MOMENT OF INSPIRATION
70" x 40", Sandy Curran, Newport News, VA

From an original painting by Robert Buvia

905. CONTEMPLATION, 62" x 69"
Diane M. DiMaria, Santa Fe, NM

906. FOREST WALK, 67" x 86"
Pat Durbin, Eureka, CA

907. RADIANT REFLECTIONS #2, 84" x 70"
Noriko Endo, Narashino, Chiba, Japan

908. ON THE WINGS OF A DREAM
63" x 64", Caryl Bryer Fallert, Paducah, KY

909. Coming Together – la Piazza
82" x 84", Laura Fogg, Ukiah, CA

910. Force of Nature, 87" x 73"
Margery O. Hedges, Kingwood, TX

911. The Perfect Flowers, 77" x 81"
Mary Ann Herndon, The Woodlands, TX

912. Dreaming Fireworks, 75" x 79"
Etsuko Iitaka, Kodaira, Tokyo, Japan

Ruth McDowell workshop

913. VISION OF HORSES, 90" x 70"
June Jaeger, Prineville, OR

914. REMEMBERING "KELLY" 84" x 56"
Shirley P. Kelly, Colden, NY

915. HELPING COUSIN EM BUILD A STRAW BALE HOUSE, 60" x 84", Dort Lee and Susan Marlier, Leicester, NC

916. 42 WINDOWS, 77" x 90"
Rhue Luna, Dallas, OR

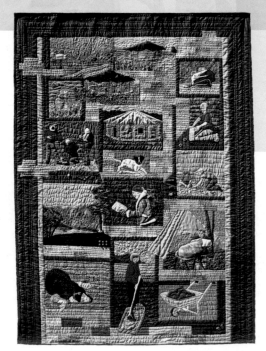

917. ANGLING, 66" x 66"
Inge Mardal and Steen Hougs
Chantilly, France

918. PANDA PERFECT DAY, 61" x 47"
Kathy McNeil, Tulalip, WA

919. PEACE MAKERS, 83" x 95"
Janet Bear McTavish and Karen McTavish
Duluth, MN

920. GRAND 1, 95" x 40"
Kathleen Ann Russu, Palm Springs, CA

Woodland Creatures Collector Series, ©Rosemary Makhan, Quilts by Rosemary

921. SEPTEMBER SONG, 62" x 72"
Carol Taylor, Pittsford, NY

922. ZIRCON AND THE WOODLAND CREATURES, 68" x 85" Ginny Vesey
Hilton Head Island, SC

1001. THE SHIRTMAKER'S VINE, 55" x 55"
Jenny Bacon, Maryborough, Victoria, Australia

1002. RAINY DAY, 45" x 59"
Yeung Ran Choung, Busan, South Korea

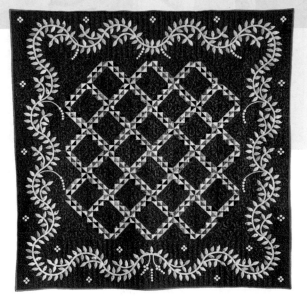

Inspired by *Hanamurasaki of Kadotamaya* woodblock print by Chobunsai Eishi, ca. 1790; appliqué technique from Suzanne Marshall

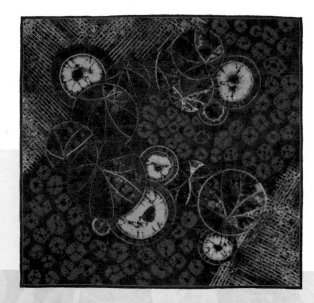

1003. In Appreciation of Yoshinori Takao, 42" x 73", Megan Farkas
Sanbornton, NH

1004. Eastern Spheres, 41" x 42"
Donna Ford, Prairie Du Sac, WI

1005. Floral Challenge, 56" x 69"
Claudia Hauch, Belvidere, IL

1006. Fragrant Chatter, 41" x 42"
Mikyung Jang, Seoul, South Korea

Floral Delight pattern, ©From my heart to your hands: Quilt Designs by Lori Smith; Leslie Gebbie workshop

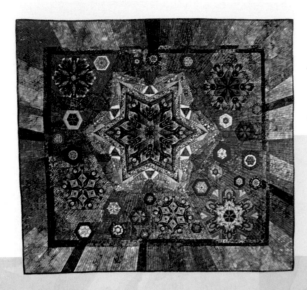

Inspired by Paula Nadelstern

Dimensional Appliqué: Baskets, Blooms, and Baltimore Borders by Elly Sienkiewicz, C&T Publishing, Inc.

1007. Starlit Night, 56" x 51"
Michael Kashey, Edinboro, PA

1008. Blue Blooms, 41" x 41"
Shirley E. Kerstetter, Spring Hill, FL

1009. Floral Fantasia, 50" x 60"
Susan Luers, Evansville, WI

1010. The Legend of Guimar, 44" x 62"
Suzanne Marshall, Clayton, MO

Auntie's Garden pattern, ©Cynthia Tomaszewski, Simple Pleasures

Design adapted from a centuries-old Norwegian tapestry

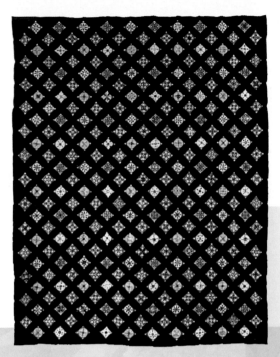

1011. JEWELER'S WINDOW, 42" x 60"
B. J. Morgan, Cullman, AL

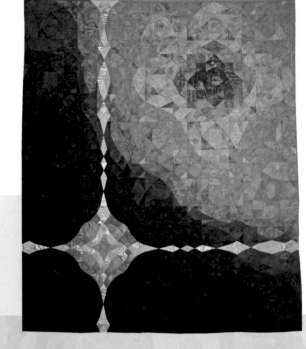

Storm at Sea block and Faceted Gem pattern from Patchwork Pattern 1000, Yoshihiro Amano, 2004; workshop with Kayoko Oguri.

1012. PRAYER AT TWILIGHT, 59" x 69"
Hisako Naito, Tokushima City
Tokushima, Japan

1013. FRACTURED HEXAGONS, 40" x 46"
Charles O'Kelley, Tuscaloosa, AL

1014. ANCIENT IMAGES: PERU, 48" x 51"
Hallie H. O'Kelley, Tuscaloosa, AL

Modified pattern from *Screen Printing for Quilters* by Hallie H. O'Kelley

Images taken on a trip to Peru

1015. SIRIUS: THE BRIGHTEST STAR
51" x 40" Young Sil Park, Incheon
South Korea

1017. PASSIONATE ROSES IN THE FOREST
46" x 64", Yoshimi Yamamoto, Itano, Tokushima
Japan

1016. MY FIRST LOVE, 54" x 52"
Junko Saito, Sapporo, Hokkaido, Japan

1018. MEMORIES OF AUTUMN, 49" x 67"
Mayumi Yoshida, Itano, Tokushima, Japan

Kayoko Oguri workshop

Needle's Eye pattern from *Encyclopedia of American Patchwork Quilts* by Kei Kobayashi,
Bunka Shuppan Kyoku, 1983; Kayoko Oguri workshop

1019. Summer Bundt Cake with Mint and Blueberries, 60" x 60"
Jane Zillmer, Mercer, WI

1101. Vines, 41" x 49"
Naomi S. Adams, Denton, TX

1102. Jack in the Pulpit, 45" x 42"
Frieda Anderson, Elgin, IL

1103. Penrose Star, 47" x 45"
Jody Aultman, Hugo, MN

1104. HAMBONE, 52" x 52"
Deborah Baldwin, Oak Park, IL

1105. ANTIQUE MAGIC, 45" x 45"
Kathryn Botsford, Campbell River
British Columbia, Canada

1106. TWELVE DAYS OF CHRISTMAS
57" x 71", Martha (Marty) Bryant
Lexington, KY

1107. FRESH AS A DAISY, 54" x 54"
Melinda Bula, El Dorado Hills, CA

Inspired by One-Book Wonders: One Fabric, One Shape, One-of-a-Kind Quilts by Maxine Rosenthal, C&T Publishing, Inc., 2006; Magic Celtic Sectional Designing, Speed Sewing by Angela Madden, MCQ Pub., 2001

1108. The 100-Year Storm, 59" x 41"
Jenny Chiovaro, Bacliff, TX

1109. Blue Footed Booby of the Galapagos Islands, 43" x 54"
Betty Cook, Joyce, WA

1110. Wait-A-Minute, 54" x 70"
Melody Crust, Kent, WA

1111. Butterfly Garden, 56" x 42"
Judi Dains, Citrus Heights, CA

1112. Crop Circles in My Stash
51" x 56", Edna Deppen, Boca Raton, FL

1113. Busy Bees & Friends, 43" x 43"
Karen Eckmeier, Kent, CT

1114. Summer Sanctuary
48" x 53", Ann Fahl, Racine, WI

1115. Stellar Stitchery, 56" x 56"
Linda S. Fletcher, Pipe Creek, TX

Pineapple Stars: Paper Piecing Patterns by Sharon Rexroad, C&T Publishing Inc., 2005

1116. A Ray of Light, 58" x 70"
Michiyo Fukumoto, Anan, Tokushima
Japan

1117. The Pleasures of Pomegranates & Poinsettias, 45" x 45", Sandra H. Gilreath
Bonaire, GA

1118. Salamander Circle Whimsy
42" x 42", Barb Gorges, Cheyenne, WY

1119. Praise Ye Now Our Gardens Green,
51" x 51", Sonia Grasvik, Seattle, WA

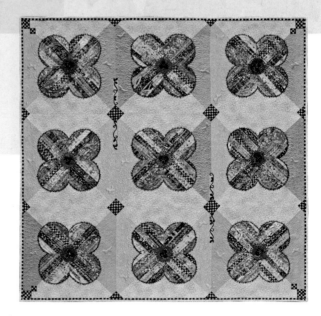

1120. The Old Homestead, 42" x 42"
Sherrie Grob, Murphysboro, IL

1121. Lost in Illusion, 41" x 48"
Gloria Hansen, East Windsor, NJ

1122. A Complete Unknown, 45" x 45"
Barbara Oliver Hartman, Flower Mound, TX

1123. Ancient Weaver, 55" x 55"
Ann Horton, Redwood Valley, CA

Patterns from *Treasury of Japanese Designs and Motifs for Artists and Craftsmen* by Carol Belanger Grafton, Dover Publications, Inc., 1983

Sunflower pattern from *Medallion Quilts: Inspiration & Patterns* by Cindy Vermillion Hamilton, American Quilter's Society, 2006

1124. TOUCHES OF THE ORIENT
50" x 50", Jaynette Huff, Conway, AR

1125. HELIOTROPIC, 53" x 57"
Nancy B. Hutchison, Kennesaw, GA

1126. CEREUS KALEIDOSCOPE
41" x 41", Margit Kagerer, Carefree, AZ

1127. MARDI GRAS II, 42" x 47"
Patricia Kerko, Sunset, SC

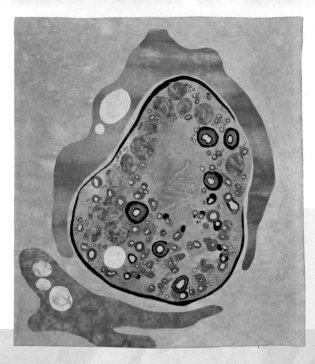

1128. Neuron II, 40" x 45"
Pamela Kirch, Cazenovia, NY

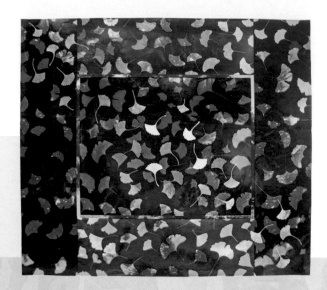

1129. Gingko Shadows, 45" x 41"
Pat Kroth, Verona, WI

1130. Calamari Time, 56" x 45"
Karlyn Bue Lohrenz, Billings, MT

1131. Tyger, Tyger, 53" x 53"
Janice Keene Maddox, Asheville, NC

1132. Koya Shadows, 59" x 42"
Jacqueline Manley, Reno, NV

1133. Feeder Defeater, 47" x 47"
Barbara Barrick McKie, Lyme, CT

1134. Worms, 40" x 45"
V'Lou Oliveira, Norman, OK

1135. Pueblo Pottery Song, 53" x 53"
Ann L. Petersen, Aurora, CO

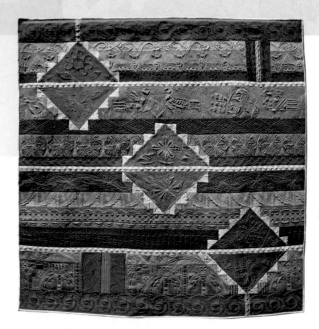

Decorative Art of the Southwestern Indians by Dorothy S. Sides, Dover Publications, Inc., 1961

1136. KING SOLOMON'S MAGICAL CARPET
41" x 54", Shulamit Ron, Kadima, Israel

1137. REALLY "WILD" FLOWERS!, 56" x 54"
Sharon L. Schlotzhauer, Colorado Springs, CO

**1138. ARIANE AT THE SEA/ARIEL,
THE SEA KING'S DAUGHTER,** 55" x 44"
Linda S. Schmidt, Dublin, CA

1139. SUNFLOWER COLLAGE, 44" x 46"
Lujean Seagal, Thousand Oaks, CA

Patterns from *Pieced Vegetables* by Ruth B. McDowell, C&T Publishing, Inc., 2002

Libby Lehman workshop

1140. Simple Pleasures, 41" x 48"
Jan Soules, Elk Grove, CA

1141. Purple Petals, 58" x 58"
Cathy Pilcher Sperry, West Chester, OH

1142. Monochrome, 46" x 60"
Susan Stewart, Pittsburg, KS

1143. Passiflora, 54" x 79"
Eileen Bahring Sullivan, Alpharetta, GA

Digitized embroidery motifs from Zundt Design Ltd. Copyright © 2000-2009, www.zundtdesign.com; Embroidery Online; and Martha Pullen Company

Indian Bonnets pattern from *Quilts Galore! Quiltmaking Styles and Techniques* by Diana McClun and Laura Nownes, McGraw-Hill, 1991

1144. KENTUCKY AUTUMN, 53" x 75"
Tess Thorsberg, Macon, GA

Indian Orange Peel pattern from *Karen K. Stone Quilts* book by Karen K. Stone, The Electric Quilt® Company 2004; border design from *Fireworks!* by Lynda Milligan and Nancy Smith, Possibilities® / Great American Quilt Factory

1145. SPICEY PICKLE, 53" x 53"
Katie Wells, Denver, CO

1146. BE HAPPY, 53" x 53"
Gisha Wogier, Kefar Yona, Israel

1147. WONDER, 42" x 45"
Kelly Wood, Lenoir, NC

Whirligig pattern from *Quilt Mavens: Perfect Paper Piecing* by Deb Karasik and Janet Mednick. American Quilter's Society, 2007

1201. DECADENT GOOSE, 50" x 70"
Candy Brown and Carla Barrett
Georgetown, CA

1202. BRILLIANT ENERGY, 50" x 50"
Betsy Carlson, Grand Rapids, MI

1203. GONE FISHING, 58" x 73"
Carolyn Carter, Addison, TX

1204. ROSES ARE RED, 57" x 77"
Regina Carter, Jackson, GA

Patterns from *The Best of Baltimore Beauties: 95 Patterns for Album Blocks and Borders* and *The Best of Baltimore Beauties, Part 2: More Patterns for Album Blocks* by Elly Sienkiewicz. C&T Publishing, Inc.

Trompe LOeil II pattern from *A New Twist on Strips 'n Curves: Featuring Swirl, Half Clamshell, Free-Form Curves & Strips 'n Circles* by Louisa L. Smith. C&T Publishing, Inc. 2007

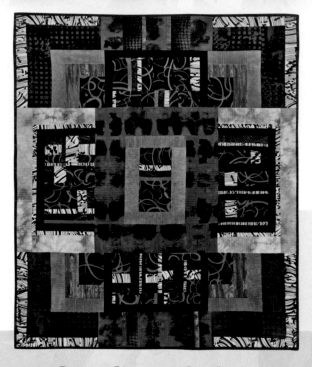

1205. BROKEN SQUARES, 48" x 56"
Marcia DeCamp, Palmyra, NY

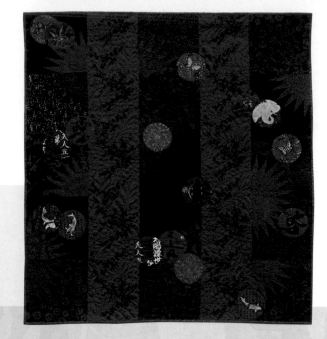

1206. HONG BAO, 43" x 47"
Dar Farmer, Dorris, CA

1207. LANIER SUNRISE, 44" x 44"
Joan Garland, Braselton, GA

1208. FASHIONABLE LADIES OF THE '20S
60" x 62", Valeta Hensley, Flemington, MO

Inner Light pattern from *Quilts with Attitude* by Deb Karasik, American Quilter's Society, 2009 ; Deb Karasik workshop

Vintage Hats & Bonnets 1770-1970: Identification & Values by Susan Langley, Collector Books: Mini magnetic calendar series of 1920s girls, Gallery Graphics, Inc.

Cosmos pattern from *Pieced Flowers* by Ruth B. McDowell, C&T Publishing, Inc., 2000; Ruth Powers workshop

1209. Santa's Block Party, 55" x 71",
Julia Kennedy and Janice Walsh
College Park, GA

1210. Do Wacka Daisy, 59" x 59"
Karen Kielmeyer, Bella Vista, AR

1211. Carousel #1, 53" x 53"
Patricia C. Kilmark, Atlanta, GA

1212. Salsa Fantasy, 42" x 41"
Kim Klocke and Mary Nordeng,
Rochester, MN

Inspired by Ricky Tims DVD

Robbie Joy Eklow workshop

1213. Rhapsody in Bloom, 56" x 56"
Susan Lanham, Brownsburg, IN

1214. Floating Blocks, 59" x 59"
Karen Laundroche, Anchorage, KY

1215. My Flower Cart, 44" x 63"
Susan McFarland, Moscow Mills, MO

1216. The Geisha and the Serving Girl
44" x 70", Claudia Clark Myers and
Marilyn Badger, Duluth, MN

1217. Pathways, 57" x 74"
Janet E. Myers, Flandreau, SD

Wild Flowers pattern from Quiltworks Today, Aug./Sept. 2004; Judy Niemeyer workshop

1218. Beautiful Blooms in My Fall Garden, 40" x 51", Judy Petersen, Pinehurst, NC

1219. Tropic Glow, 50" x 50"
Joyce Stewart and Ann Seely
Deweyville, UT

1220. Ocean Dream, 40" x 40"
Lisa Walton, Sydney, Australia

Aunt Millie's Garden: 12 Flowering Blocks from ©Piece O'Cake Designs by Becky Goldsmith and Linda Jenkins, C&T Publishing, Inc. 2008

Embroidery designs inspired by Hatched in Africa

1221. Peacock Fantasy, 53" x 53"
Charlotte Wright, Stillwater, OK

1301. Incommunicato, 54" x 54"
Esterita Austin, Port Jefferson Station, NY

1302. White Orchids, 42" x 48"
Rosalie Baker, Davenport, IA

1303. Digilily, 43" x 40"
Deborah Baldwin, Oak Park, IL

With permission of composer/musician Michael Blake

1304. Making Music, 41" x 50"
Mary Barry, Vacaville, CA

1305. Dranandra in the Fall
46" x 69", JoAnn Belling, Des Moines, IA

1306. Classic American Dolls, 50" x 50"
Linda Reuss Benson, Mequon, WI

1307. EIEIO, 49" x 46"
Nancy S. Brown, Oakland, CA

Stamps reproduced with permission of U.S. Postal Service

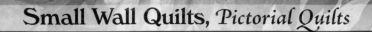

1308. Splendor in the Grass, 59" x 41"
Melinda Bula, El Dorado Hills, CA

1309. Monstera, 53" x 70"
Betty Busby, Albuquerque, NM

1310. Metamorphosis, 58" x 44"
Sandy Curran, Newport News, VA

1311. To Market, 41" x 42"
Mary Diamond, Interlaken, NY

1312. ALMOST TIME TO GO, 40" x 50"
Rebecca Douglas, Punta Gorda, FL

1313. BEGONIA PICOTEE LACE
50" x 41", Pat Durbin, Eureka, CA

1314. CAPTIVATED, 57" x 44"
Maria Elkins, Beavercreek, OH

1315. POPPIES ON ICE, 54" x 68"
Grace J. Errea, Laguna Niguel, CA

Inspired by The Whistling Season by Ivan Doig. Houghton Mifflin Harcourt, 2006

1316. TUNDRA COMET, 59" x 40"
Judy Eselius, Lake Oswego, OR

1317. TRANQUILITY, 42" x 44"
Lou Ann Estes, Oak Island, NC

1318. EGYPTIAN WATER GARDEN II
45" x 70", Ann Fahl, Racine, WI

1319. HEIGHT OF TULIP SEASON
43" x 56", Laura Fogg, Ukiah, CA

1828 line drawing from Treasures of Egypt and Nubia by Ippolito Rosellini, Grange Books, U. K.

Sunflowers and Leaves patterns by J. Phil Beaver

1320. GROWING WILD, 51" x 55"
Donna Ford, Prairie Du Sac, WI

1321. SNAPSHOT SHANNON'S BANTAM
45" x 63", Denise Tallon Havlan, Plainfield, IL

1322. HIDE 'N SEEK (NOW WHERE DID THAT MOUSIE GO?), 51" x 47", Annette M. Hendricks Grayslake, IL

1323. FIELD OF LILIES, 48" x 62"
Charlotte Hickman, Oklahoma City, OK

Inspired by *Pieced Flowers* by Ruth B. McDowell, C&T Publishing, Inc., 2000

Ruth B. McDowell workshop

1324. SWAMP CRITTERS, 46" x 59"
Daphne Huffman, Dallas, TX

1325. ORANGE HIBISCUS, 56" x 58"
Mary R. Keasler, Cleveland, TN

1326. SUNFLOWER TURNING, 44" x 70"
Jacqueline Manley, Reno, NV

1327. THE CALM AFTER THE STORM, 49" x 49"
Inge Mardal and Steen Hougs, Chantilly, France

1328. THE HARE'S VERSION, 41" x 42"
Barbara Barrick McKie, Lyme, CT

1329. CROSSING CALAMITY CREEK, 59" x 74"
Kathy McNeil, Tulalip, WA

1330. MIZUBASHO, 52" x 64"
Hiroko Miyama, Chofu City, Tokyo, Japan

1331. MARTINI POODLE, 44" x 55"
V'Lou Oliveira, Norman, OK

The Infinite World of M. C. Escher by J. L. Locher, Abradale/Abrams, 1984

1332. Confusion, 55" x 46"
Nancy Parmelee, Sonoma, CA

1333. Spring Encounter, 46" x 40"
Ruth Powers, Carbondale, KS

1334. Little Red, 55" x 80"
Kimberly Rado, Encinitas, CA

1335. Green Pastures, 42" x 53"
Mary Lou Ridley, South Haven, MI

Adapted from a leather tooling by Chris Jenson of a copyrighted pattern from Tandy Leather Factory, Inc.

Kayoko Oguri workshop

1336. SHELTER ME, 45" x 42"
Pat Rollie, Los Angeles, CA

1337. SHINING WATER SURFACE, 51" x 67"
Hideko Ryuki, Tokushima City, Tokushima, Japan

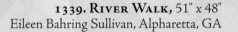

1338. FACADE, 42" x 52"
Melissa Sobotka, Richardson, TX

1339. RIVER WALK, 51" x 48"
Eileen Bahring Sullivan, Alpharetta, GA

1340. Grandmother's Legacy
43" x 57", Gail E. Thomas
Vernon, British Columbia, Canada

1341. Transect Zones, 46" x 55"
Karen Reese Tunnell, Atlanta, GA

1342. Etui, 57" x 55" Irène Van Tonder,
Kyalami, Gauteng, South Africa

1343. Love, 51" x 41"
Marilyn H. Wall, West Union, SC

Marilyn Belford workshop

1344. Sprouts #2, 41" x 43"
Laura Wasilowski, Elgin, IL

In the style of Alphonse Mucha

1345. Harvest, 45" x 53"
Jennifer Wheatley-Wolf, Arlington, VA

1401. The Gift, 57" x 57"
Debra Archer and Diane Schotl
Maplewood, MN

1929 mural art by John Gabriel Beckman, Casino at Avalon, Catalina Island, California

1402. The Island of Romance, 40" x 61"
Louise Allyn Beckman, Vancouver, WA

Circle-Play: Simple-Designs for Fabulous Fabrics by Reynola Pakusich,
C&T Publishing, Inc., 2004

1403. COLORS OF TOBAGO, 49" x 49"
Maud Bentley, Rowley, IA

1404. THE PATH NOT TAKEN, 45" x 42"
Sherryl Buchler, Scottsdale, AZ

1405. SNAILS IN PARADISE, 54" x 69"
Betty Cook and Deborah Steinhour
Joyce, WA

1406. SWIMMING IN CIRCLES, 56" x 71"
Carolyn Coonrod, Shell Knob, MO

Lady Liberty block from Karen K. Stone Quilts by Karen K. Stone, The Electric Quilt®
Company, 2004

1407. Whispers on a Hot Summer Day
58" x 84", Véronique Diligent, Chirnside Park
Victoria, Australia

1408. Stirred Not Shaken, 43" x 43"
Mary Dyer, Merritt Island, FL

1409. Atchison, Topeka, and The Santa Fe II, 56" x 49", Deb Fitzpatrick
Longmont, CO

1410. Nova, 59" x 59", Linda S. Fletcher
Pipe Creek, TX

Feathered Goose pattern, ©Judy Niemeyer, Quiltworx.com

Inspired by antique quilts

1411. Cooked My Goose, 59" x 59"
Tammy Gardner, Edwardsburg, MI

1412. Hex Medallion, 58" x 58"
Norene D. Goard, Hendersonville, NC

1413. Purple Haze, 44" x 46"
Lee Hart, Meadville, PA

1414. Tie Quilt #2, 54" x 62"
Lynn Isenburg, Saint Louis, MO

Photo not available

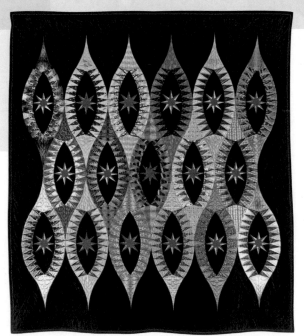

Jewel pattern by Jacqueline de Jonge, becolourful.com

1415. Hanging in the Balance
59" x 65", Kathleen V. Allingham Johnson
St. Albert, Alberta, Canada

1416. Nasturtiums, 51" x 46"
Pamela Johnson, Monterey, MA

1417. Night Fisher, 44" x 65"
Dian Keepers, Centralia, WA

1418. A Valentine to Remember
58" x 72", Norma J. Koelm, Albuquerque, NM

J. Phil Beaver workshop

Album Quilt pattern from *Appliqué Album Quilts* by Melanie Fabian and Sandra Sigal.
Gick Publishing Inc., 1983

The Quick and Easy Giant Dahlia Quilt on the Sewing Machine by Susan Aylsworth Murwin and Suzzy Chalfant Payne, Dover Needlework Series, Dover Publications, Inc., 1983

1419. LAKE HOUSE DAHLIA, 57" x 57"
Robin Meyer, Mableton, GA

1420. HEADWATERS, 55" x 54"
Gay Young Ousley, Abilene, TX

1421. STORM WARNING, 55" x 50"
Shirley Prakke, Johannesburg, Gauteng
South Africa

1422. HEARTFUL DAYS, 40" x 40"
Aki Sakai, Hachioji, Tokyo, Japan

Appliqué Rose Garden: Vintage Album Patterns by Faye Labanaris, American Quilter's Society, 2005; Award-Winning Appliqué Birds by Pamela Humphries, American Quilter's Society, 2007

Charlotte Warr Andersen workshop

1423. WELCOME TO SUE AND ED'S GARDEN, 51" x 51", Pat Scheideler-Kern and Linda James, Whispering Pines, NC

1424. THE FOREST ORCHID, 40" x 49"
Donna Severance, Pembroke, NH

1425. HARMONY, 41" x 48"
Amy Joy Talbot, Grand Junction, CO

1426. HOMAGE, 59" x 58"
Mary Vaneecke, Tucson, AZ

Based on photo taken by artist's niece, Emily M. Lutz

Inspired by Susan McCord's 1880s Vine Quilt

1501. OBSESSION, 10" x 10"
Diane Becka, North Bend, WA

1502. DRESDEN CHARMS, 16" x 16"
Kathryn Botsford, Campbell River
British Columbia, Canada

1503. PINEAPPLE PLEASURES, 13" x 13"
Elaine Braun, Paducah, KY

1504. SHADES OF ROYALTY, 9" x 9"
Kathy Downie, Richmond, IL

A miniature version of Ida Tendam's quilt from *Pineapple Quilts: New Quilts from an Old Favorite* edited by Barbara Smith, American Quilter's Society

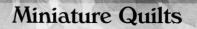

1505. Violinist, 17" x 17"
Maria Elkins, Beavercreek, OH

1506. Little Autumn, 24" x 24"
Shoko Ferguson, Clinton, MD

1507. Miniature Pineapple, 11" x 13"
Janet Frank, Tallahassee, FL

1508. Mission: Impossible 2,
12" x 12", Kumiko Frydl, Houston, TX

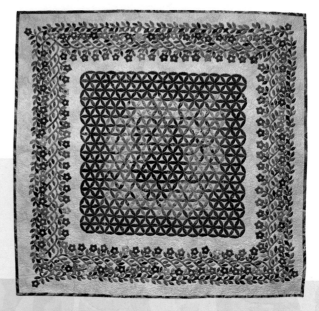

1509. Little Rosie Mae, 19" x 19"
Bill Fullerton, Branson, MO

1510. Peter Pan, 12" x 11"
Sue Holdaway-Heys, Ann Arbor, MI

1511. Enchanted, 16" x 16"
Jane Holihan, Walworth, NY

1512. Pink Elephants Too
14" x 14", Pat Holly, Ann Arbor, MI

Antique embroideries from India were Pat's inspiration

1513. DIAMONDS, 16" x 23"
Rita Hutchens, Sandpoint, ID

1514. GINGKOS, 10" x 10"
Pat Kroth, Verona, WI

1515. SAFFRON OFFSPRING, 14" x 14"
Barbara E. Lies, Madison, WI

1516. FASCINATING GARDEN, 20" x 20"
Hiroko Miyama, Chofu City, Tokyo, Japan

Decorative Flower and Leaf Designs by Richard Hofmann, Dover Publications, Inc., 1991

Inspired by an antique quilt

Happy Villages: Step into a Fabric Collage Adventure! by Karen Eckmeier, The Quilted Lizard, 2007; Nancy Mambi workshop

1517. MINI LEAVES AND CHAINS
21" x 21", Mary-Margaret Morton
Ann Arbor, MI

1518. MY TOWN, 22" x 22"
Suzanne O'Brien, New Richmond, WI

1519. RAINY DAY STAR, 11" x 11"
Lorraine Olsen, Springfield, MO

1520. HOUSTON FRIENDS, 24" x 24"
Laura B. Parks, Batesville, AR

Rainy Day Star pattern from *Little Lone Star Quilts: Sew Perfect Points Every Time; Exciting New Paper-Piecing Techniques* by Lorraine Olsen, C&T Publishing, Inc., 2009

Inspired by a pressed-tin ceiling design from the Hemingway-Pfeiffer Museum in Piggott, Arkansas

Crazy Quilt Stitches by Dorthy Bond, self-published 1981; and Treasury of Crazyquilt Stitches by Carole Samples, American Quilter's Society, 1999

Based on Joan Leahy Blanchard's quilt WILD GOOSE CHASE

1521. MEMORIES OF SHANNON
14" x 14" Diana Perry, Hot Springs, AR

1522. GEESE GALORE, 15" x 18"
Mary Sanko, Danvers, IL

1523. QUILTER'S UTOPIA: WHERE FABRIC GROWS ON TREES, 12" x 12"
Sharon L. Schlotzhauer, Colorado Springs, CO

1524. DUSK A L'ORANGE, 13" x 13"
George Siciliano, Lebanon, PA

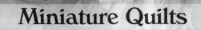

1525. THREADS OF GOLD, 12" x 12"
Mildred Sorrells, Macomb, IL

1526. A BIT DOTTY - CRAZY QUILT, OF COURSE, 16" x 16", Sandra Starley, Moab, UT

1527. VINTAGE, 12" x 12"
Suzy Webster, Apple Valley, MN

A

Abe, Hisae....................17
Adams, Naomi S. 59
Akemi, Tajima....................34
Aliu, Esther....................34
Anderson, Frieda....................59
Arai, Tomoko....................26
Archambault, Brenda....................49
Archer, Debra....................87
Ashley, Bobbie....................17
Ashworth, Hazel....................23
Aultman, Jody....................59
Austin, Esterita....................76

B

Bacon, Jenny....................54
Badger, Marilyn....................46, 74
Baker, Rosalie....................76
Baldwin, Deborah....................60, 76
Barrett, Carla....................71
Barry, Mary....................77
Basket, Cherry....................24
Baugher, Annabel....................4
Becka, Diane....................94
Beckman, Louise Allyn....................87
Behrens, Cindy....................18
Belford, Marilyn....................49
Belling, JoAnn....................77
Benson, Linda Reuss....................77
Bentley, Maud....................88
Bethesda Quilters....................23
Black, Barbara....................13
Blair, Sheila D.....................42
Bluhm, Irena....................14
Botsford, Kathryn....................60, 94
Braun, Elaine....................94
Brown, Candy....................71
Brown, Nancy S.....................77
Bryant, Martha (Marty)....................60
Buchler, Sherryl....................88
Bula, Melinda....................60, 78
Burnham, Barbara M.....................14
Busby, Betty....................78
Buschauer, Georgina....................18
Buvia, Mary S.....................49
Byrum, Michele....................43

C

Campbell, Susan....................46
Carlson, Betsy....................71
Carter, Carolyn....................71
Carter, Regina....................71
Cartwright, Clara....................18
Cavanaugh, Dawn....................45
Chalmers, Mary....................11
Chiovaro, Jenny....................61
Choi, Eun Young....................34
Choung, Yeung Ran....................26, 54
Collins, Dot....................43
Collins, Peg....................43
Cook, Betty....................61, 88
Coonrod, Carolyn....................88
Coughlin, Joanne....................24
Crine, Deb....................43
Crust, Melody....................61
Cunningham, Jan....................14
Curran, Sandy....................49, 78
Cushman, Rosemary....................44

D

Dains, Judi....................61
de Jonge, Jacqueline....................44
DeCamp, Marcia....................44, 72
Delaney, Kathy....................14, 44
Deppen, Edna....................62
Diamond, Mary....................78
Diligent, Véronique....................89
DiMaria, Diane M.....................50
Donohue, Darlene....................15
Douglas, Rebecca....................79
Downie, Kathy....................94
Doyle, Terri....................45
Durbin, Pat....................50, 79
Dyer, Mary....................89
Dyken, Linda....................4

E

Eberle, Gail....................18
Eckmeier, Karen....................62
Eklow, Robbi Joy....................45
Elias, Gina....................45
Elkins, Maria....................79, 95
Endo, Noriko....................50
Errea, Grace J.....................79

Eselius, Judith....................80
Estes, Lou Ann....................80

F

Fackler, Brian....................48
Fahl, Ann....................62, 80
Fallert, Caryl Bryer....................50
Farkas, Megan....................55
Farmer, Dar....................72
Ferguson, Shoko....................95
Fisher, Helen....................24
Fitch, Karen....................26
Fitzpatrick, Deb....................89
Fletcher, Linda S.....................62, 89
Fogg, Laura....................51, 80
Ford, Donna....................55, 81
Frank, Janet....................95
Frazer, Jan....................35
Frydl, Kumiko....................95
Fujiwara, Junko....................4
Fukumoto, Michiyo....................63
Fullerton, Bill....................96
Funaki, Kumiko....................4, 35

G

Garcia, Cindy....................15
Gardner, Tammy....................90
Garland, Joan....................72
Garwood, Peggy....................5
Gilbert, Donna....................5
Gilreath, Sandra H.....................11, 63
Goard, Norene D.....................90
Goda, Hiroko....................26
Goodwin, Cindi....................35
Gorges, Barb....................63
Graber, Miriam....................25
Grasvik, Sonia....................63
Griffiths, Gwenfai Reese....................27
Grob, Sherrie....................64
Guthrie, Karen L.....................27

H

Haase, Elisabeth Polenz....................15
Hansen, Gloria....................64
Hansen, Sharon....................19
Hara, Mieko....................27
Hart, Lee....................90

Hartman, Barbara Oliver.......................64
Hata, Kayoko 27
Hauch, Claudia.............................55
Haukom, Mary M. 19
Havlan, Denise Tallon.....................81
Hawkins, Kristi 18
Hedges, Margery O. 51
Hempen, Patti.............................35
Hendricks, Annette M. 81
Hensley, Valeta............................72
Herndon, Mary Ann.....................51
Hickman, Charlotte 81
Hirano, Hatsune..............................5
Hirasawa, Akemi 28
Hire, Dianne S. 36
Holdaway-Heys, Sue......................96
Holihan, Jane...............................96
Holly, Pat....................................96
Horton, Ann..................................64
Hosoo, Noriko.............................36
Hougs, Steen 53, 82
Huff, Jaynette...............................65
Huffman, Daphne.........................82
Hutchens, Rita 97
Hutchison, Nancy B. 65

I

Iitaka, Etsuko................................51
Ikuma, Yuriko.............................28
Inagaki, Kyoko............................28
Isenberg, Lynn 11, 90
Ishinami, Katsumi 36
Itoyama, Kumiko 36

J

Jaeger, June.................................52
James, Linda................................93
Jang, Mikyung.............................55
Johnson, Hope...............................5
Johnson, Kathleen V. Allingham ...91
Johnson, Page..............................16
Johnson, Pamela..........................91
Johnson, Patricia 45
Jordan, Jolana A. 37
Joyner, Gay.................................19
Junko Sawada Group 24

K

Kagerer, Margit 65
Kandler, Georgianne 37
Kashey, Michael 56
Kashizaki, Masae 37
Katsuno, Yachiyo...........................6
Keasler, Mary R. 82
Keaton, Dolores 19
Keepers, Dian 91
Keith, Laurel 43
Kelley, Kathy.................................6
Kelly, Shirley P. 37, 52
Kennedy, Julia 73
Kerko, Patricia 65
Kerstetter, Shirley E. 56
Kessi, LuAnn 38
Kido, Noriko.................................6
Kielmeyer, Karen 73
Kilmark, Patricia C. 73
Kingston Heirloom Quilters 24
Kirch, Pamela 66
Kitada, Ikuyo 28
Kitami, Yoshiko 29
Klocke, Kim 73
Knapp, Janet...............................15
Knapp, Susan Brubaker 38
Koelm, Norma J. 91
Kordek, Fran 11
Korengold, Barbara........................6
Kroth, Pat.............................66, 97
Kumagawa, Masako 7

L

Lambert, Julie Yaeger 12
Lanham, Susan.............................74
Laundroche, Karen 74
Lee, Chungsu 29
Lee, Dort....................................52
Leichner, Sandra 38
Lewis, Jan...................................38
Lies, Barbara E. 97
Lohmar, Jean...............................12
Lohrenz, Karlyn Bue.....................66
Luers, Susan................................56
Luna, Rhue 52

M

Maddox, Janice Keene 66
Maezawa, Yoshiko 7
Magee, Sally................................20
Manley, Jacqueline.................67, 82
Mardal, Inge.........................53, 82
Marlier, Susan..............................52
Marshall, Suzanne 56
Martin, Nancy Sterrett 39
McCarty, Sue...............................46
McDonald, Margaret 46
McFarland, Susan.........................74
McGibbon, Linda.........................46
McKie, Barbara Barrick 67, 83
McNeil, Kathy.......................53, 83
McTavish, Janet Bear....................53
McTavish, Karen..........................53
McVay, Lou Ann..........................25
Measels, Karen S. 20
Meyer, Gloria..............................48
Meyer, Robin...............................92
Miyake, Takako 7
Miyama, Hiroko 83, 97
Mizuno, Megumi 7
Morgan, B. J. 57
Morishita, Shizuyo.................8, 29
Morton, Judy Laval.......................25
Morton, Mary-Margaret.................98
Munkelwitz, Kathy.................16, 29
Murphy, Sharon 37
Myers, Claudia Clark 46, 74
Myers, Janet E. 75

N

Naito, Hisako...............................57
Nakano, Mariko 30
Nakao, Yukiko 30
Nakazawa, Felisa 39
Napier, Diana 20
Naylor, Philippa 39
Nordeng, Mary 73
Noto, Kazuko..............................12
Nuehring, Keith A. 20

O

O'Brien, Suzanne.........................98
Ohkawa, Fumiko 8

Oiwa, Hitomi 30
Okamatsu, Taeko 39
Okamoto, Chizuko......................30
O'Kelley, Charles........................57
O'Kelley, Hallie H. 31, 57
Oliveira, V'Lou 67, 83
Olsen, Lorraine..........................98
Onuma, Uiko..............................31
Oosawa, Mariko..........................31
Ousley, Gay...............................92
Ozaki, Miki...................................8

P

Park, Young Sil 58
Parks, Laura B. 98
Parmelee, Nancy 84
Parrott, Peggy 40
Peck, Katheryn 21
Perkes, Gina..............................47
Perry, Diana 99
Persing, Barbara.........................47
Petersen, Ann L. 67
Petersen, Judy 75
Pinner, Meri 25
Polston, Barbara.........................25
Poplin, Elaine Wick......................40
Powers, Ruth 84
Prakke, Shirley...........................92

R

Rado, Kimberly 84
Radtke, Marsha D. 8
Reese, Jerre 12
Rego, Leslie...............................47
Reynolds, Sherry 21, 40
Ridley, Mary Lou 84
Rollie, Pat 85
Ron, Shulamit 68
Roy, Linda 9
Russu, Kathleen Ann 53
Ryuki, Hideko 85

S

Saito, Junko 58
Sakai, Aki 92
Sammis, Nancy 16
Sanko, Mary...............................99

Scheideler-Kern, Pat.....................93
Schillig, Beth 13
Schlieckau, Sharyl.......................47
Schlotzhauer, Sharon L. 68, 99
Schmidt, Linda S. 68
Schotl, Diane 87
Schroeder, Mary C. 40
Seagal, Lujean 68
Sebens, Norde 31
Second Friday Quilters, ...24
Seely, Ann 75
Severance, Donna 93
Sherman, Mark 16
Shier, Katalin R. 16
Shinozaki, Taeko.........................21
Siciliano, George 99
Simpson, Lori 16
Sobotka, Melissa 85
Sorrell, Carole 21
Sorrells, Mildred 13, 100
Soules, Jan 69
Sperry, Cathy Pilcher 69
Spiering, Vicki 13
Starley, Sandra 100
Steinhour, Deborah 88
Stewart, Joyce............................75
Stewart, Susan 48, 69
Stoll, Lydia 25
Stone, Karen K. 41
Sugyama, Akemi 9
Sullivan, Eileen Bahring............... 69, 85
Sutoh, Mitsuko 32

T

Takahashi, Yuko 32
Takasaki, Mitsuyo........................22
Takemoto, Kyoko 32
Takeyama, Yasuko........................32
Takido, Fusako 9
Talbot, Amy Joy 93
Tanaka, Junko 33
Tareishi, Yukiko and Friends 25
Taylor, Carol 41, 54
Thomas, Gail E. 86
Thompson, Nadine..........................9
Thorsberg, Tess 70
Tope, Teri Henderson 33

Tsuchiya, Kinuko.........................33
Tsukatani, Natsuko.......................22
Tunnell, Karen Reese....................86

U

Umemoto, Yoshimi 33

V

Van Tonder, Irène 86
Vaneecke, Mary 93
Vernex, Pierra 22
Verroca, Rita 10
Vesey, Ginny 54
Vierra, Kristin 17

W

Wall, Marilyn H. 86
Walsh, Janice.............................73
Walton, Lisa 75
Wasilowski, Laura 87
Watanabe, Akiko 22
Watanabe, Yasue.........................23
Webb, Debi 23
Webb, Joann 10
Webster, Suzy 100
Wells, Katie 41, 70
Werlich, Sandra C. 41
West, Melanie 42
Wetzler, Rachel 42
Wheatley-Wolf, Jennifer 87
Wogier, Gisha 70
Woo, Eunhee 42
Wood, Kelly 70
Woodworth, Judy 48
Wright, Charlotte 17, 76

Y

Yamada, Naoko 10
Yamamoto, Kayoko 34
Yamamoto, Yoko 10
Yamamoto, Yoshimi......................58
Yoshida, Mayumi 58

Z

Zillmer, Jane..............................59
Zimmer, Sally 48
Zimmerman, Kathryn 48

100-Year Storm, The 61
25th Wedding Anniversary 32
322 Treehouse Lane 18
42 Windows 52

A

All Creatures Great & Small 27
Almost Time to Go 79
Always a Bloom in My Garden 23
Ancient Images: Peru 57
Ancient Weaver..................................64
Angling 53
Animal Book...7
Anniversary 28
Antique Magic.....................................60
Aquatic Circles 37
Ariane at the Sea/Ariel, the Sea King's
    Daughter 68
Atchison, Topeka, and the
    Santa Fe II 89
Autumn Joy...45
Autumn Splendour 24

B

Ballet 36
Be Happy 70
Beautiful Blooms in My
    Fall Garden....................................75
Begonia Picotee Lace 79
Bella Rose 17
Between the Lines................................41
Beyond Sky 30
Big Bang, The......................................46
Birds 'n Urns.......................................14
Birds of a Feather 15
Bit Dotty – Crazy Quilt,
    of Course, A..................................100
Black Lace...37
Bloomin Beauty...................................18
Blossom of My Life 21
Blue Blooms..56
Blue Footed Booby of the Galapagos
    Islands 61
Blue Land 28
Blue Merle (Circle Log Cabin) 20
Bouquet for Mr. Tims 35
Breath of Spring, A..............................28

Bright Future of Daughters...................32
Brilliant Energy 71
Broken Squares 72
Brown Bird's Lullaby............................20
Busy Bees & Friends............................62
Butterflies in the Garden 5
Butterfly Garden 61

C

Calamari Time.....................................66
Calendula 40
Calm after the Storm, The 82
Camellia of Art Deco 24
Camp Fire 42
Captivated 79
Carousel #1 73
Cereus Kaleidoscope 65
Challenge I 18
Charisma...13
Chorus of Angels 7
Circle Parade 22
Clam Session 41
Classic American Dolls........................77
Color of Matsuri
    (Japanese Festival), The.................22
Colorado Sunrise Sunset 41
Colors of Tobago.................................88
Colorwash Garden 18
Coming of Spring, The 30
Coming Together – la Piazza 51
Complete Unknown, A..........................64
Concerto in the Night Sky, The 31
Confusion..84
Contemplation.....................................50
Cooked My Goose................................90
Crop Circles in My Stash 62
Crossing Calamity Creek......................83
Crowning Glory 12
Crystal Blue Baskets 16
Cutwork Appliqué................................12
Cwlwm Lafant.....................................27

D

Decadent Goose..................................71
Development 28
Diamonds..97
Digilily 76

Do Wacka Daisy 73
Doormats #1..44
Dragon Star 48
Dranandra in the Fall 77
Dream Land...29
Dream Story 33
Dreaming Fireworks.............................51
Dresden Charms 94
Dusk a L'Orange..................................99

E

Eastern Spheres...................................55
Egyptian Water Garden II 80
EIEIO 77
Enchanted 96
Endless World II, The 6
Etui 86

F

Facade 85
Fantasy in Lace 49
Fascinating Garden..............................97
Fashionable Ladies of the '20s.............72
Feeder Defeater 67
Festival of the Night Sky, The 12
Field of Lilies 81
First We Take Manhattan 21
Fish of Rainbow Colors........................24
Floating Blocks 74
Floating Lilies Along the Water 9
Floral Beauty.......................................19
Floral Challenge 55
Floral Fantasia 56
Florentine Window 23
Flower & Birds I 34
Flower Carnival....................................30
Flower Seeds of Happiness...................23
Flowers in Aqua 4
Flowing Counterpoint 47
Flying 26
For All My Companions 31
Force of Nature 51
Forest Orchid, The 93
Forest Walk...50
Forest Walks 26
Forever Spring 4
Forever Yours......................................48

Four Seasons of Wonderment...........19
Fractal Blue Rose 35
Fractured Hexagons 57
Fragile World, The...............................48
Fragrant Chatter 55
Fresh As a Daisy 60
Fruit of the Loom 33

G
Galaxy 27
Galaxy of Nostalgic Snails 15
Garden Frost...45
Geese Galore...99
Geisha and the Serving Girl, The........74
Gift, The 87
Gingko Shadows...................................66
Gingkos 97
Glittering Summer Garden...................36
Gloria's Garden.....................................48
Glory of Ancient Remains 26
Gone Fishing 71
Gradation Log Cabin #7....................... 8
Grand I 53
Grandmother's Legacy 86
Green Pastures 84
Growing Wild 81
Guilford, CT, ca 1950 49

H
Hambone 60
Hanging in the Balance.........................91
Hare's Version, The...............................83
Harmony 5
Harmony 93
Harvest 87
Hawaiian Cross.....................................25
Headwaters 92
Healing Rose Hip 33
Heartful Days 92
Hearts & Flowers..................................45
Height of Tulip Season.........................80
Heliotropic..65
Hell Freezes Over 46
Helping Cousin Em Build a Straw Bale
          House 52
Hex Medallion 90
Hibiscus 12

Hibiscus in Hawaiian Breeze 10
Hide 'n Seek (Now Where Did That
          Mousie Go?)...............................81
Homage 93
Honey, I'm Home 5
Hong Bao 72
Houston Friends....................................98

I
I Love Waikiki 7
iCandy 3.0...45
In Appreciation of Yoshinori Takao 55
In My Garden.. 9
In Praise of Wool 11
Incommunicato.....................................76
Indiana Starburst 25
Island of Romance, The 87
Istanbul's Flower 17

J
Jack in the Pulpit..................................59
Jeepers...It's Jane! 13
Jesus, the True Vine..............................15
Jewel Nouveau......................................16
Jeweler's Window 57
Journeys 46
Joyful Journey 13
Just Because Revisited 17

K
Kentucky Autumn 70
King Solomon's Magical Carpet............68
Komorebi... 8
Koya Shadows.......................................67

L
Laced Lokelani 7
Lake House Dahlia................................92
Lanier Sunrise 72
Latte Obsession.....................................15
Legend of Guimar, The.........................56
Listen with Your Eyes 44
Little Autumn..95
Little Red...84
Little Rosie Mae....................................96
Lost in Illusion 64
Love...86

M
M.E.C. Remembered 14
Making Music 77
Mardi Gras II 65
Martini Poodle 83
Maryland Beauty...................................23
Medea Escaping 49
Memories 26
Memories of Autumn 58
Memories of Shannon 99
Metamorphosis 78
Mini Leaves and Chains 98
Miniature Pineapple 95
Miraflores 41
Mission: Impossible 2 95
Mizubasho 83
Moment of Inspiration, The 49
Monochrome 69
Monstera 78
Monsteriosity..35
Moondance 42
Morning Glory Madness 10
Morning Has Broken 40
Morning Sunshine 22
Mother-Daughter Redwork..................25
Moulin Rouge.......................................17
Mountain Holly and the Rare
          Red-Berried Mistletoe 14
Multiple Personalities 35
Murphy's Star 4
My Favorite Monstera........................... 6
My First Love 58
My Flower Cart 74
My Kind of Fun 13
My Lovely Susie 30
My Rose Garden 44
My Town..98
My Wyoming Valley..............................40

N
Nasturtiums...91
Neuron II 66
New York, New York 38
Night Fisher...91
Nova..89

O

Obsession 94
Ocean Dream 75
OLD Homestead, The 64
On Spaceship 39
On the Wings of a Dream 50
Orange Hibiscus 82
Oriental Dahlia 34
Oriental Fantasy 43

P

Paisleys and Peacocks, India 19
Panda Perfect Day 53
Papercuts and Toile 44
Passiflora 69
Passion 33
Passionate Roses in the Forest 58
Path Not Taken, The 88
Pathways 75
Peace Makers 53
Peacock Fantasy 76
Penrose Star 59
Perfect Flowers, The 51
Peter Pan 96
Pineapple Pleasures 94
Pink Elephants Too 96
Pink Petal Party 38
Playing Rats 36
Pleasures of Pomegranates &
        Poinsettias, The 63
Poppies on Ice 79
Praise Ye Now Our Gardens Green 63
Prayer at Twilight 57
Precious Hopes 8
Precious Moments 36
Pueblo Pottery Song 67
Pueblo Rain 37
Purple Haze 90
Purple Petals 69

Q

Quilter's Utopia: Where Fabric
        Grows on Trees 99

R

Radiant Flowers 10
Radiant Reflections #2 50

Rainbow Pyramid 21
Rainy Day 54
Rainy Day Star 98
Ray of Light, A 63
Really 'Wild' Flowers! 68
Red and Green Redux 11
Remembering "Kelly" 52
Remembering Rose 43
Resurrection of Spring 47
Return to the Attic 8
Reynolds Crossing 21
Rhapsody in Bloom 74
River Walk 85
Rondo of Roses 27
Rose and Star Waltz 34
Roses Are Red 71
Roses of Shenandoah 10

S

Saffron Offspring 97
Salamander Circle Whimsy 63
Salsa Fantasy 73
Sampler, The 47
Santa's Block Party 73
Seasons 43
September Song 54
Seven Black Birds 11
Sew Is Life 6
Shades of Royalty 94
Shelter Me 85
Shining Water Surface 85
Shirtmaker's Vine, The 54
Simple Pleasures 69
Simply Mandalas 22
SIRIUS: The Brightest Star 58
Snails in Paradise 88
Snapshot Shannon's Bantam 81
Snowball's Chance 37
Soleil 39
Special Rose 9
Spicey Pickle 70
Splendor in the Grass 78
Spring Encounter 84
Sprouts #2 87
Starlit Night 56
Stars Over Agrabah 6
Stellar Stitchery 62

Stirred Not Shaken 89
Storm Warning 92
Summer Bundt Cake with Mint and
        Blueberries 59
Summer Sanctuary 62
Sundance 43
Sunflower Collage 68
Sunflower Turning 82
Sunflowers 38
Sunshine & Shadow 34
Swamp Critters 82
Sweet Bouquet 32
Sweet Candy Dots 20
Sweet Memories Are Forever in
        My Heart, The 32
Swimming in Circles 88
Synchronized Dance 14

T

Tale of Korean Thimble Golmu 29
Tamoto huri huri 29
Tea with Miss D 38
This Old Thing 40
Threads of Gold 100
Tie Quilt #2 90
To Market 78
Touches of the Orient 65
Tranquility 80
Transect Zones 86
Treasures in the Sea 39
Tribute to Tolkien 46
Tropic Glow 75
Tropical Beauties 31
Tropical Beauty 5
Tropical Radiance 42
Tundra Comet 80
Tuscan Sun 47
Twelve Days of Christmas 60
Tyger, Tyger 66

V

Valentine to Remember, A 91
Varsity Medley 24
Victorian Pinks 16
Vines 59
Vintage 100
Vintage Button Bouquet 9

Violinist 95
Vision of Horses 52

W
Wait-A-Minute 61
Walk in the Forest 31
Walk in the Meadow, A 25
Wedding Rings for Mavis and CJ 11
Welcome Present, A 4
Welcome to Sue and Ed's Garden 93
What Will Be, Will Be! 42
Whimsey 29
Whispers on a Hot Summer Day 89
White Gold 39
White Orchids 76
Wings and Feathers 16
Wonder 70
Worms 67
Woven-Wind Flowers 19

Y
Ye Ole Celtic Cottages 20

Z
Zircon and the Woodland Creatures .. 54

2011 AQS Quilt Show & Contest – Rules

1. The maker(s) of a cloth quilt can enter a completed quilt by submitting entry blank, entry fee, and images of the completed work.

2. Limit of two entries per entrant(s) or group, one entry per category. Those listed as "other stitchers on this quilt" may also have their own two entries.

3. Quilt must be constructed and/or stitched and quilted by person(s) named on entry blank.

4. Quilts constructed and/or stitched by one or two persons can be entered in all categories except Category 5. Quilts constructed and/or stitched by three or more people can only be entered in Group Category 5.

5. All quilts must be quilted by hand, by machine, or both.

6. Quilt must have been finished between January 1, 2009, and January 1, 2011, and be in excellent condition.

7. Quilts winning cash awards in any previous AQS contests (Paducah, Nashville, Knoxville, Lancaster or Des Moines), or quilts made from precut or stamped kits are ineligible.

8. Quilts must be a single unit and not framed with wood, metal, etc.

9. Quilts in categories 4 and 14 must be a first-time entry for any stitchers on the quilt in any AQS contest (Paducah, Nashville, Knoxville, Lancaster or Des Moines).

10. Pictorial quilts (representation of a person, place, or thing) must be entered in category 9 or 13, depending on size.

11. Quilt Sizes: (Actual quilt size must fit dimensions listed for category.) All quilts must have the rod pocket sewn ½" from the top edge for hanging. For more information on the sleeve requirements, see Sleeve Info at www.AmericanQuilter.com under Shows & Contests. A label identifying the maker must be stitched or securely attached to the back lower edge of each quilt.

    a. Bed-sized quilts in categories 1 – 5 must be 60" to 110" in width and a length of 80" or more.

    b. Large wall quilts, categories 6 – 9, must be 60" to 110" in width and a length of 40" or more.

    c. Small wall quilts, categories 10 – 14, must be 40" to 60" in width and a length of 40" or more.

    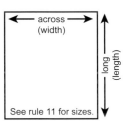

    d. Miniature quilts in category 15 must be a maximum of 24" in width and length. Miniature quilts can be any style, including pictorial, that are appropriately reduced in scale. Sleeves are not needed on miniature quilts.

12. Quilt entries in categories 1–9 will be considered for the Janome Best of Show, AQS Hand Workmanship, BERNINA Machine Workmanship, and Gammill Longarm Machine Quilting purchase awards. Quilts in categories 10–14 are eligible for the Moda Best Wall Quilt purchase award. Quilts in category 15 are eligible for the Benartex Best Miniature purchase award. These purchase awards will become a part of the permanent collection of the The National Quilt Museum. Winners not wishing to relinquish their quilts may retain possession by refusing their prize money. Photography and printing rights must still be granted to AQS.

13. Quilt must be available for judging and display from April 8, 2011, through one week after the show.

14. Incomplete, torn, or soiled quilts will not qualify for entry or exhibition.

15. Full-view digital photo must show all edges of the finished quilt. Detail photo must show the quilting stitches. Do not send slides.

16. All decisions of the jurors and judges are final. AQS reserves the right to reject any entry, including those that fail to follow the quilt contest rules.

17. Please include the complete name and e-mail address of your local newspaper so a news release can be sent there.

18. See Categories for descriptions of each category.

To enter, send:

(a) Completed and signed entry blank with correct category selected, brie description, techniques used, quilting method, and source of pattern design.

(b) Send two digital quilt images with **no modification** including croppin and color correction (one full view of **completed** quilt and one detail completed piece) on a CD-ROM, using a minimum of 4 MP (megapixel camera, on **highest resolution setting, saved as a JPEG or TIFF file** (*sure to finish the CD* and label the disk with your name and title of th work). Send only one entry per CD-ROM. If you have photos or slides your work, you can save them on a CD-ROM using your computer or your local photo processing center. Photos cannot be e-mailed, and CD will not be returned. Identifying name(s) must NOT be visible on the qui in the images.

(c) Include a photo of the entrant(s) on the CD-ROM, so it will be availab for the *American Quilter* magazine if you are a winner. The photo shoul include full face, head, and shoulders only. See additional informatio under Suggestions for Good Quilt Photography on page 4 of these rules.

(d) Entry fee:
   AQS members: $10.00 per quilt
   Non-members: $30.00 per quilt

Categories

Bed Quilts – width 60" to 110"; length 80" or more
1. Bed Quilts – Hand Quilted – quilting technique is by hand
2. Bed Quilts – Home Sewing Machine – predominant quilting technique is by home sewing machine
3. Bed Quilts – Longarm/Midarm Machine – predominant quilting technique is by longarm/midarm machine
4. 1st Entry in an AQS Quilt Contest – any technique
5. Group – any technique; made by three or more people

Large Wall Quilts – width 60" to 110"; length 40" or more
6. Large Wall Quilts – Hand Quilted – quilting technique is by hand
7. Large Wall Quilts – Home Sewing Machine – predominant quilting technique is by home sewing machine
8. Large Wall Quilts – Longarm/Midarm Machine – predominant quilting technique is by longarm/midarm machine
9. Pictorial Quilts–representation of a person, place, or thing – any technique

Small Wall Quilts – width 40" to 60"; length 40" or more
10. Small Wall Quilts – Hand Quilted – quilting technique is by hand
11. Small Wall Quilts – Home Sewing Machine – predominant quilting technique is by home sewing machine.
12. Small Wall Quilts– Longarm/Midarm Machine – predominant quilting technique is by longarm/midarm machine.
13. Pictorial Quilts–representation of a person, place, or thing – any technique
14. 1st Entry in an AQS Quilt Contest – any technique

Miniature Quilts – width 24" maximum; length 24" maximum
15. Miniature – all aspects of the quilt are in reduced scale

(Written judging evaluations are provided for each quilt exhibited at this show.)

2011 AQS Quilt Show & Contest – Paducah

Send in this entry form with CD-ROM, *Appraisal, and
*Design Permissions (*if applicable). This form may be photocopied.

☐ Member **$10.00** • Membership Number _____

☐ Non-Member **$30.00**

Entrant(s) or Group Name _____
(Please Print)   (ONLY THESE Name(s) will be used in the Show Book)

Street _____

City _____ State _____ Country _____ Zip or Postal Code _____

Phone _____ Cell _____ E-mail _____

Contact the city desk or feature editor at your newspaper to get an e-mail address; newspapers are requesting e-mailed press releases.

Complete Name of Newspaper _____ Newspaper E-mail _____

Select Your Category Number (see rule 11 for more information):

Bed Quilts:
W 60" to 110"; L 80" or more
☐ 1. Hand Quilted
☐ 2. Home Sewing Machine
☐ 3. Longarm/Midarm Machine
☐ 4. 1st Entry – AQS Contest
☐ 5. Group

Large Wall Quilts:
W 60" to 110"; L 40" or more
☐ 6. Hand Quilted
☐ 7. Home Sewing Machine
☐ 8. Longarm/Midarm Machine
☐ 9. Pictorial Quilts

Small Wall Quilts:
W 40" to 60"; L 40" or more
☐ 10. Hand Quilted
☐ 11. Home Sewing Machine
☐ 12. Longarm/Midarm Machine
☐ 13. Pictorial Quilts
☐ 14. 1st Entry – AQS Contest

Miniature:
24" maximum, W and L
☐ 15. Miniature

Information About Your Entry:

Title _____ Size in inches _____ " across by _____ " long

Approx. Insurance Value $ _____ (Over $1,000 requires a written appraisal **included with this form**. Maximum value is $5,000.)

Name(s) of everyone who stitched on this quilt: _____

Brief Description of Quilt for Show Book (25 words) _____

Techniques: (Choose all that apply)
☐ Appliqué   ☐ Piecing   ☐ Embroidery   ☐ Trapunto
☐ Needlework Technique _____   ☐ Other _____

Quilting: (Choose all that apply)   ☐ **Hand**   ☐ **Home Sewing Machine**   ☐ **Longarm/Midarm Machine**   ☐ **Embroidery Machine**
     ☐ With Stitch Regulator   ☐ With Stitch Regulator
     ☐ Computer-Assisted Stitch Software

Design Pattern Source: (Choose all that apply: Use separate paper for additional space.)
☐ Totally Original (Definition: first, not a copy of a previous work; new creation; patterns by others are NOT used.)
☐ Pattern(s) used; list pattern source (if any patterns were used, please list them below.)
☐ Design inspired by another source (please list source of inspiration below).

Magazine	Issue	Year	Project Title
Pattern/Book title – List complete title	Author	Publisher	Project Title
Other Artwork title/type		Contact Information for artist, publisher, or source	
Workshop Title		Workshop Instructor	

Signature _____

Please put your name on the CD-ROM and mail digital images (as outlined in the rules), completed entry blank, and fee for each quilt to:

**American Quilter's Society,
Dept. 2011 Paducah Contest Entry,
PO Box 3290, Paducah, KY 42002-3290
BY JANUARY 3, 2011**

Credit Card (Visa, MasterCard, or Discover)

Card Number ☐☐☐☐-☐☐☐☐-☐☐☐☐-☐☐☐☐   Exp. Date ☐☐☐☐   Ver. Code ☐☐☐   Check # _____

AQS presents the sponsors for the 26th Annual Quilt Show & Contest. Each category and event is sponsored by a company in the quilting industry. To open the show, company representatives present the cash awards at the Awards Presentation on Tuesday, April 20, evening.

Best of Show . . . . **Janome America, Inc.**

Hand Workmanship Award . . . . **American Quilter's Society**

Machine Workmanship Award . . . . **BERNINA of America, Inc.**

Longarm Machine Quilting Award . . . . **Gammill Quilting Systems**

Best Wall Quilt Award . . . . **Moda Fabrics**

Wall Hand Workmanship Award . . . . **Coats & Clark**

Wall Machine Workmanship Award . . . . **Brother International Corporation**

Wall Longarm Workmanship Award . . . . **Handi Quilter**

Best Miniature Quilt . . . . **Benartex, Inc.**

Judges Awards . . . . **American Professional Quilting Systems**

Bed Quilts

    Hand Quilted . . . . **Superior Threads**

    Home Sewing Machine . . . . **EZ Quilting by Wrights/Simplicity Creative Group**

    Longarm / Midarm Sewing Machine . . . . . . **Hobbs Bonded Fibers**

    1st Entry in AQS Quilt Contest . . . . **Morgan Quality Products**

    Group Quilt . . . . **Mettler**

Large Wall Quilts

    Hand Quilted . . . . **Fairfield Processing Corporation**

    Home Sewing Machine . . . . **Baby Lock USA**

    Longarm / Midarm Sewing Machine . . . . . . **Robert Kaufman Co., Inc.**

    Pictorial Quilts . . . . **Elna USA**

Small Wall Quilts

    Hand Quilted . . . . **FreeSpirit/Westminster Fabrics**

    Home Sewing Machine . . . . **Koala Cabinets**

    Longarm / Midarm Sewing Machine . . . . . . **Hoffman California Fabrics**

    Pictorial Quilts . . . . **Husqvarna Viking**

    1st Entry in AQS Quilt Contest . . . . **YLI Corporation**

Miniature Quilts . . . . **Benartex, Inc.**

Event Sponsors . . . . **Baby Lock USA, Ken's Sewing Center, Quilt In A Day**

Lecture Series . . . . **Pfaff**

Fashion Show . . . . **AQS, Hobbs Bonded Fibers, BERNINA of America, Inc.**

General Sponsors . . . . **ABM International; A1 Quilting Machines; AccuQuilt; Amazing Designs; Horn of America; Pellon/Legacy; HQ Pro-Stitcher; Jenny Haskins Designs; Nolting; Rotary Club of Paducah; Statler Stitcher; TinLizzie 18; Tracey's Tables**

AQS/Hinterberg Quilt Show Giveaway . . . . **Hinterberg Design**

Workshops . . . . **BERNINA of America, Inc., Elna USA, Handi Quilter, Janome America, Inc.,**

The National Quilt Museum Workshop Series . . . . **Flynn Quilt Frame Co., Janome America Inc., Olfa Corporation**

The National Quilt Museum New Quilts from an Old Favorite Contest: Sunflower

    Clover Needlecraft, Inc., Moda Fabrics, Janome America, Inc.,

School Block Challenge . . . . **Flynn Quilt Frame Co., Janome America, Inc., Olfa Corporation**